BOOKS, PUPPETS AND THE MENTALLY RETARDED STUDENT

By

John and Connie Champlin

Illustrated by Carol A. Anderson

Special Literature Press

Omaha, Nebraska

Published in the United States of America by

Special Literature Press
P. O. Box 4397
Benson Station
Omaha, NE 68104

ISBN 0-938594-00-1

To our parents,

Lawrence and Loretta Champlin

Mike and Helen Kelly

FOR THEIR LOVE AND ENCOURAGEMENT

Acknowledgements

Many thanks are due to our students who often experienced the trial-and-error methods of our literature teaching.

To our special aunt, Anna Brazzell, our sincere appreciation and warm affection for her continuous support.

To Mr. Spencer Shaw of the University of Washington we say "thank you" for his interest in this project.

To Nancy Renfro for her generous advice and kind encouragement which were often needed and always appreciated, we give our love.

To Area Education Agency 13, Council Bluffs, Iowa, for its technical assistance, we extend our appreciation.

To our friend Marilyn R. Skinner--typist, librarian, and special educator--we express our warmest regards.

Appreciation to Mirra Ginsburg and Macmillan Publishing for their permission to adapt Mushroom in the Rain.

CONTENTS

Preface

During our years of working in the classroom and library, we have continuously been faced with the problem of how to introduce literature meaningfully to the mentally retarded student. At first we searched for books to give youngsters for independent reading, only to find that they put the books down too soon and without understanding.

Reading to the students was a step forward, but even here we found difficulties with vocabulary, concepts, and interest. Finally the search for "the method" of teaching literature led to "active participation." This opened up many possibilities, including: story-sharing, choral speaking, puppetry, creative dramatics, art, music, . . .

This book takes several areas and integrates them into, what we believe to be, a practical "how-to" sequence. The first sections survey rationale and techniques for working with the mentally retarded student specifically in the area of literature. The remainder of the book illustrates the various means of sharing literature to further the mentally retarded student's understanding and enjoyment.

IDENTIFYING

the MENTALLY RETARDED STUDENT

Legislation throughout the country is changing the status of the handicapped. State and federal legislation (e.g., The Education for All Handicapped Children Act of 1975) now mandate special education programs, and integration of handicapped students into regular programs when appropriate.

Search for Materials

Librarians and special education teachers are increasingly searching for materials and methods to enable the mentally retarded student to understand and enjoy the world of literature at his/her level. At the university level, schools of library science and schools of education are exploring for ways to increase competencies of their students with regard to the handicapped.

"Educable" Equals "Mild"

This book centers on one category of the handicapped population--that of the educable mentally retarded. This category of handicap denotes the mildest form of mental retardation. The terms "educable mentally retarded," and "mildly mentally handicapped" will be used interchangeably within this book.

Specific Characteristics of Learning/Behavior

Intellectual Functioning
Intellectual functioning, as measured by an intelligence test is a main factor in determining whether a student is retarded. If a student scores significantly below average on an individual intelligence test (e.g., Wechlser Intelligence Scale for Children, Stanford-Binet) he/she may be eligible for placement in a special education program for the mentally retarded.

Depending on the student's intelligence quotient (IQ score) and other criteria, he/she may be placed in a program for the mildly or educable mentally retarded, the moderately or trainable mentally retarded, or the severely mentally retarded.

Comprehension
The educable mentally retarded student experiences some difficulty in comprehending school subjects within the regular curriculum. He/she will not understand concepts and relationships to the same degree as the average student. Because the retarded student will always find the regular curriculum subjects difficult, he/she will increasingly fall behind in school due to the cumulative arrangement of learning on which most curricula are based.

Special education programs, however, utilize curricula specifically developed for the retarded student's rate of learning and long-term goals. Still, the student's learning rate will always be below that of his average peer.

Language   During the intermediate grades of 4, 5, and 6, the mildly retarded student will be two to four years below age-expectation in language skills. Usually this student will have more ability to understand language aurally (receptive language) than he/she does in speaking language orally (expressive language).

Reading, in terms of calling words, will also be two or more years below grade level by intermediate grades.

Attention Span   Retarded students seem to have shorter attention spans during on-task assignments than do their average peers. Since verbal ability is a serious weakness, these students often become frustrated or inattentive when made to listen to excessive verbal teaching or, what appears to them to be, uninteresting lessons.

Memory   Medium- and long-term memory is a decided problem area which hampers these students in learning. Teaching of concepts through a variety of materials, and frequent repetition is usually necessary.

Arithmetic

By intermediate age, most students will be able to perform rational counting to 100 or higher and to solve simple addition and simple subtraction problems. Consumer skills such as money value, change-making, and price-comparison shopping will demand much teaching time throughout school.

Abstractions

The ability to think logically--to follow sequences, to use deductive and inductive reasoning, will be difficult for these students. The use of concrete objects and the use of demonstrations in teaching will assist in the understanding of abstract concepts.

Variability

These are only general characteristics and, of course, there will be much variance from one student to another in terms of any one characteristic. At the same time, if you realize the types of difficulties which the student is likely to experience, you will be better prepared to teach him/her in the classroom and the library.

RATIONALE and TECHNIQUES
of SHARING LITERATURE

This Thing Called "Literature"

Why? What value does literature have for mentally handicapped students? Is it practical, feasible for students with mental handicaps . . . students who will always have a difficult time learning? Would it be better to forget such a dif-ficult goal as that of teaching "literature?"

Shakespeare
Christie
Dr. Seuss What does it include? Most people would grant that it's a very broad category of writing and story-telling.

It might be Dickens or Shakespeare
for you, but Twain, Sandoz, and Christie
for your best friend. For your
child or your student, he/she may
prefer Steig or Blume, while my child
may love the Brothers Grimm and Dr.
Seuss.

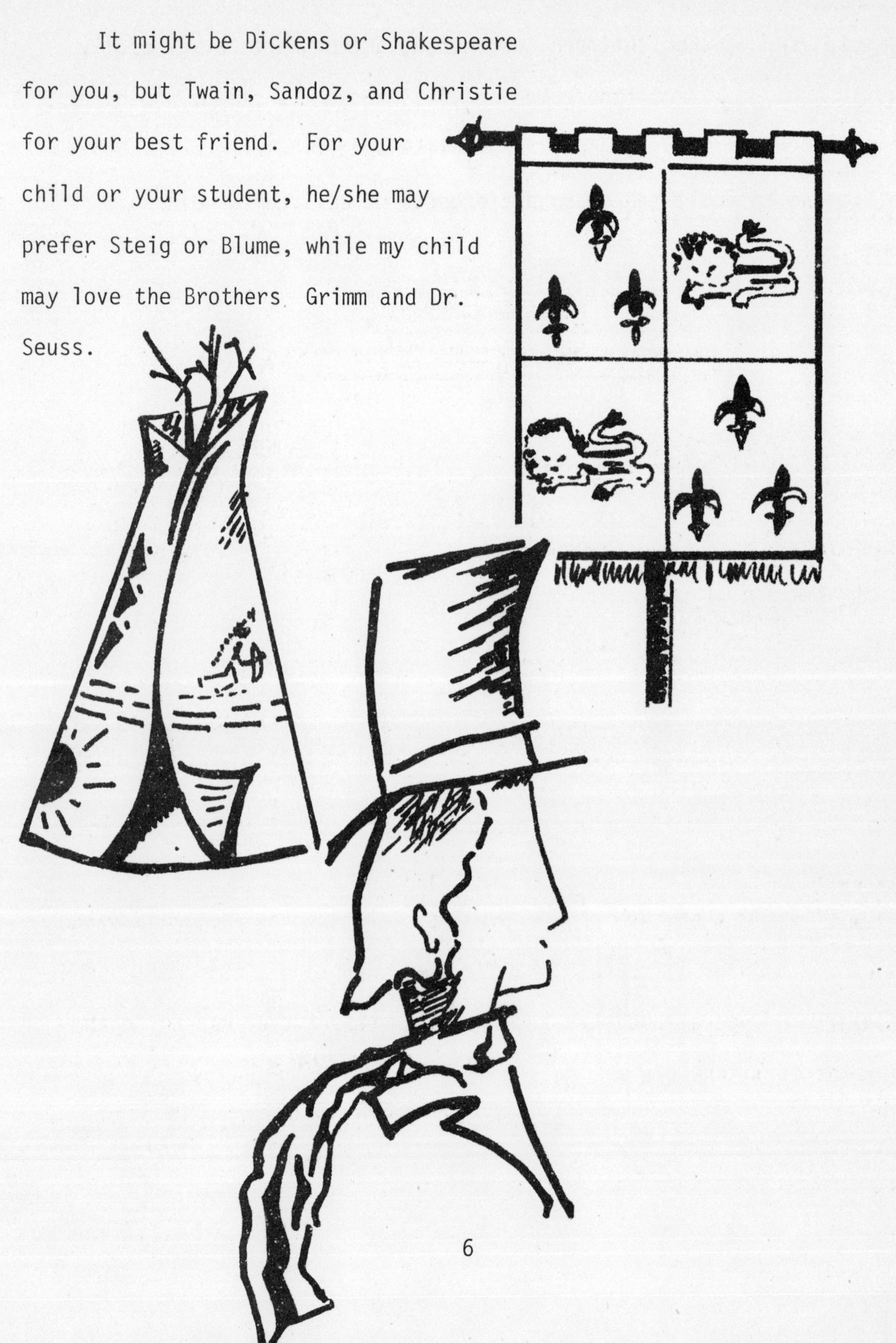

For children, of course, authors are not generally
important. The critical factor is simply whether
they understand and like a particular story. And
who's going to fault the story preferences of a five-year old anyway?

Rather than become involved with the concept of good and
poor literature, let's agree that people must begin some-
where, and that's obviously wherever they may be in the
enjoyment of literature.

It doesn't matter whether I'm a five-year old enjoying <u>The</u> <u>Cat</u> <u>in</u> <u>the</u> <u>Hat</u> for the hundredth time, or a fifteen-year old mentally retarded youth listening and liking that story for the first time. In either case I'm at that level of development in literature where I'm able to understand and enjoy <u>The</u> <u>Cat</u> <u>in</u> <u>the</u> <u>Hat</u>. If the story is literature for the five-year old, then it remains literature when the fifteen-year old mentally handicapped youth listens as well.

Understand
and
Enjoy
their conflicts.

Literature gives us enjoyment in the reading, telling, or hearing of it. Our minds understand the story and our emotions become involved with the characters and

Vocabulary
Characters
Sequence

Comprehension, of course, is often the main problem of the mentally retarded student in school subjects. And literature comprehension is no exception!

"Understanding" for our students means knowing the vocabulary, discerning the difference between characters, being aware of sequence, and relating cause and effect. These factors are chiefly abstractions, and that's what makes it difficult for mentally handicapped persons who must rely greatly on concrete objects to understand.

On the other hand, there exists much literature which mentally handicapped persons can understand and enjoy, even though they may not be able to read it.

Setting Goals and Objectives

| Planning Objectives | Deciding upon objectives and programming for students to meet these objectives is a major step in being successful with mentally retarded students. Having |

Planning
Objectives

Deciding upon objectives and programming for students to meet these objectives is a major step in being successful with mentally retarded students. Having objectives for students in our minds or written on paper forces us to plan our story and program accordingly.

Without such forethought, we wouldn't know if we're really being successful or merely wishing success. Often there's a world of difference between the two!

Meeting
Objectives

If we decide to "teach sequence of characters" as our current objective of a small group, we know exactly what to expect from our students and, in turn, what we must do in preparation. If our story is <u>The Three Billy Goats Gruff</u>, the student must go away knowing that the small Billy Goat Gruff was first to cross the bridge, etc. Further, we must think and decide upon the way the student is going to prove to us that he/she knows what the objective requires.

Is he/she going to point to the picture of the first, second, and third goats to cross the bridge, or is he/she going to tell us the names of the first goat, the second goat, etc.?

As you progress through the succeeding chapters, appropriate objectives will be suggested. Also, as you become better acquainted with your students' needs and abilities, you will be able to formulate suitable goals for your particular students.

Problems and Solutions

Our students have problems which are universal enough to give them mention, though it should be recognized that not all students will exhibit all problems. Nor will offered solutions be equally successful with all students.

Problem:
Abstractions
Difficult

Mentally handicapped students lack the capability of forming and retaining concepts with the same ease as average students. New vocabulary, for example, will have little meaning if merely defined verbally. Note how difficult the concepts of "yesterday" and "the day after tomorrow" are to understand because there is nothing that can be seen or touched (that is, there is no concrete object) as "yesterday." Such abstractions create unusually difficult times for our students.

Solution:
Concrete
Objects

One alternate to merely defining or describing new vocabulary is to use concrete objects whenever possible. A "concrete object" may be the real object itself or models of it. Let the student handle the object, use it appropriately, say its name, and ask questions about it.

When real objects are not available, pictures may help explain an object. You and the students may explore that picture as part of your introduction.

Problem: Attention Span Short	It frequently happens that retarded students lose interest quickly. Yet much may be done to improve and maintain the students' attention.

Solution: Shorten Periods	Try preventive medicine here. Instead of the usual thirty minute lesson of the average class, try a fifteen or twenty-minute period. As the students

attend better and longer, lengthen the session accordingly.

Solution: Tell Students Expectations	Often we presume that students know what is expected. Too often they really don't understand because behavioral expectations have not been

clearly detailed for them. For example, tell them that they're expected to sit quietly and listen to the story. Further, let them know that

those who sit quietly for the five-minute story will be able to help
the librarian/teacher put the filmstrip projector away at the end of
the period, etc. Such rewards are very helpful with initially hard-
to-handle students.

**Solution:
Switch
Activities**   Having several short activities (which may or may
not be related) rather than one long activity will
likewise help hold the students' interest. For
example, when teaching <u>The Three Billy Goats Gruff</u>, the first five
minutes could be spent in review of the story, the next ten minutes
given to practice of the different sounds of "trip-trap" of the three
goats and the "Who's that crossing over my bridge?" of the troll. Take
the last ten minutes to practice sequencing of first, second, and third
by having the students line up in sequential order.

14

It's important that you tell the students when they are doing well. Be honest but generous with your praise. Even Sally who constantly jitters in her seat must have a few seconds of attentiveness. During those times you might say, "I see you're really trying to sit still, Sally. That's great!"

Sometimes just a chance to stretch, walk across the room, or otherwise be physically active will break potential periods of inattentiveness. Try it and be surprised!

Problem: Memory, of course, correlates and is part-and-parcel
Memory   of the mentally handicapped student's problem. How
Poor   can we help the student to remember during literature
study?

Solution: Decide beforehand what is necessary for the student to
Stress   understand in a story, or whatever other objectives
Important   you may have. Too often we make the mistake of drill-
ing on subject matter which is unnecessary to our specific objectives.

Solution: Decide beforehand what you expect of your students in
Explain or   terms of demonstrating their knowledge. Is it suf-
Memorize?   ficient that they explain in their own words what
has happened, or do you expect a word-for-word recall? Remember that
utilizing one's own words in explanation illustrates a high degree of
understanding!

Solution: Once you've determined what's necessary for your stu-
Teach in   dents to know, break the task into reasonable units.
Units   If you're sharing a story and want general feedback,
ask the students to tell what happened on that one page. If the students
are expected to memorize, break the line into phrases and teach accordingly.

Solution:
Repetition
Vary your questions to derive the same answer. Or ask the same question at intervals throughout the session until you're sure the students are remembering or understanding. An interesting strategy is for you to make a game of important facts by giving the students a choice of answers. For example, "Who said, 'Now I'm coming to gobble you up?' the Big Billy Goat Gruff or the Troll?" Watch the hands go up!

Problem:
Conclusions
Difficult
Our students have a very difficult time with generalizations and drawing conclusions. One of the major objectives of teaching literature should be to help develop these processes.

Solution:
Present
Alternatives

Present two solutions to a problem that a character in a story is experiencing. Make one answer more logical or plausible than the other. Ask the student to choose the answer that makes sense to him/her. Together turn the page to see if the student's choice was correct. If the student's choice was incorrect, quietly explain why the other choice was a little better, but praise honestly for his/her attempt. If that student chooses the less logical choice again, make the choices presented even further apart in logical thinking.

Solution:
Leading
Questions

The basis for drawing conclusions is from known facts. Therefore, be sure the students know needed facts before asking a question which requires deduction or inference. As you read The Three Billy Goats Gruff, ascertain whether the students understand the facts of the story by asking, "What do the goats have to cross in order to get to the hillside?" and "Who lives

under the bridge?"

     With these two facts in mind, the students will be able to answer

with greater probability, "What trouble do you think the goats are

likely to meet?" The answer requires a bit of thought based on the

two obstacles already mentioned. But you've neatly built up to the

point of having the students view the bridge and the troll as potential

obstacles.

Caution: Questioning is an extremely valuable technique to use
Watch   in helping the students think ahead and draw conclu-
Didactism   sions. Yet we don't want to make this period so

didactic that the students don't enjoy the story. This is such an

important caution, that it will pop up throughout the book.

     As you work more and more with mentally handicapped students these

solutions to potential difficulties will become second nature!

Baskin, Barbara & Karen H. Harris. The Special Child in the Library.
     Chicago: American Library Association, 1976.

     A collection of articles which examines aspects of the rela-
tionship between the library and the special child. The sections
on materials utilization and programming offer many useful ideas.

Payne, James S. et al. Exceptional Children in Focus. Columbus, Ohio:
     Charles E. Merrill, 1974.

     Small paperback which gives brief overviews of handicapped
groups, relevant statistics, and educational programs.

Pointer. Washington, D.C.: Heldref Publications, 3 times yearly.

     A journal designed to promote successful practices and approaches
for educating special education students in the least restrictive
environment. Each issue has a theme. Articles are based on actual
experiences and include examples and illustrations of the approach
being advocated. A sample theme, "Creative Approaches to Helping
the Classroom Teacher."
     Order from: Heldref Publications, 4000 Albemarle St., N.W.,
Washington, D.C. 20016. $15.00 yearly.

Teaching Exceptional Children. Reston, Virginia: Council for Excep-
     tional Children. Quarterly.

     Articles often present practical ideas/strategies for working
with mentally retarded students. Classroom teachers contribute
tested techniques to the feature, "Teacher Idea Exchange." Order
from: The Council for Exceptional Children, 1920 Association
Drive, Reston, VA 22091. $12.50 yearly.

SELECTING

BOOKS and STORIES

One of the chief problems for the librarians who teach mentally retarded students has been a dearth of books which the mentally retarded student is able to read independently. Yet, even an enormous increase in books with low reading levels will not be sufficient to enable this special student to read independently.

There are other factors and problems involved, other than just "the right book." Through this chapter and the next, some of the problems of merely giving this student a book and expecting him/her to read, will present themselves.

Main Thesis — Rather than speak to many specific books which this student can read, we're going to state a generalization.

A mentally handicapped student will be able to understand and enjoy a book or story to the extent that the librarian/teacher does the following:

1) selects books with regard to certain criteria and

2) adapts books in certain ways.

<table>
<tr><td>

Non-
Reader

</td><td>

Let's talk about our students' probable capabilities in the world of reading and literature.

</td></tr>
</table>

Non-Reader

Let's talk about our students' probable capabilities in the world of reading and literature.

For all practical purposes our audience is functionally unable to read library books which are of interest and at its intellectual level. We are not saying these students cannot read at all, for surely many intermediate students can read within the primary grades level. But they clearly are unable to read at their interest levels. Being unable to read for the purpose of enjoying literature might appear to put a damper on the entire process of literature study. Not so!

Group Sharing

While your student, Joe, has reading needs as an individual student, the emphasis in this book is on group-sharing with literature. The reason for such a group orientation is that a mentally handicapped student needs more than just the physical fact of a book. That individual also requires: an introduction to the book, knowledge of new concepts and vocabulary, understanding of happenings, and the background to enjoy the story. After having engaged in this group process, the individual may find the reading of that book a more meaningful experience.

Listening Comprehension

As stated previously, one factor in our student's favor is that he/she understands at a considerably higher level than at which he/she can read. Listening comprehension is a big plus for this student. Eleven-year-old Joe, for example, understands quite well about Homer Price's unfortunate mishap with the doughnut machine when I read the story aloud, so let's rate him about fourth grade level in "listening comprehension."

Interest Level

Now let's find out what topics or types of stories interest him. Does he like only humor or would he also enjoy an historical biography or a sports story?

To find out, we might sit down with him and ask what he likes to do, what stories he likes to hear over and over, what television shows he likes to watch. Such an informal survey will be exceedingly helpful since a lot of guesswork will be eliminated with regard to his

interests. In fact, it's such important information that we would
probably write it down and keep it for future use.

Interest
is a Start

With this general interest information, we can begin
our search for stories for Joe. While this information, appeal of humorous stories, is necessary, we
still have to choose from the many humorous books available. And that's
where specific selection criteria come in!

Criteria for Selection-Fiction

There are four critical factors to consider when choosing books to share with mentally retarded students. These considerations include: maturity of content, simple plot, representational illustrations, and understandable text. This last point, understandable text, is necessary only if you want to read verbatim from the text. As you'll see in the next chapter, there are ways around an inappropriate text.

Maturity of Context

Maturity of content or age-appropriate matter, means that the subject matter and illustrations should be appropriate to the student's actual age level. For a twelve-year-old student, Peter's Pocket by Barrett is inappropriate for two reasons.

First, the content about pockets and what can go into them (children's favorite objects) is not of interest to a twelve-year-old. Secondly, the illustrations show a preschool child as the main character-- again it would be inappropriate for a twelve-year old to be talked down to in such a manner.

25

Simple
Plot

Another consideration is that the plot be simple, yet strong. Too many concurrent themes may result in confusion or misunderstanding. Julius Scheer's <u>Rain</u> <u>Makes</u> <u>Applesauce</u> is an example of a story with too much--too many illustrations, too many minor themes. Compare the Scheer book with <u>The</u> <u>Three</u> <u>Billy</u> <u>Goats</u> <u>Gruff</u> for strength, and Mirra Ginsburg's <u>Mushroom</u> <u>in</u> <u>the</u> <u>Rain</u> for simplicity.

Representational
Illustrations

With picture books or easy books, illustrations need to be generally representational. The more abstract the picture, the more difficult for your audience to understand.

And, of course, simple, large and uncluttered drawings are best.
Authors/illustrators who usually produce simpler illustrations aid our
students in comprehension of the story. Examples of such illustrators
include: Ezra Jack Keats, Marcia Brown, Roger Duvoisin, Pat Hutchins,
and Tomi Ungerer.

As with any good picture book, the illustrations should provide
continuity of the story to such a degree that it would be largely understandable without the text.

No	A very serious problem encountered in picture book
Younger	selection for the intermediate student is the presence
Children	of "much-younger" children in books which otherwise

might be appropriate. Having a child as the hero or main character
who is noticeably younger than the mentally retarded reader creates a
couple of difficulties.

The first is that the reader may come to identify himself/herself
with that younger child. The danger is that inappropriate behavior
or an unrealistic self-image might be fostered. A second difficulty
is that the reader may realize that the child is younger and may
reject "reading" not only that book, but also others you may offer.

Text	If we expect our students to understand the text of a book
	as written, the text must be simple, brief, and fast-
	moving. While the librarian/teacher will read the text,

the concepts within the story must be within the students comprehension
abilities.

Criteria for Selection--Non-Fiction

The purpose of sharing non-fiction with handicapped students is
somewhat different than that for sharing fiction. The main difference
is that non-fiction (viz., nature, science, fine arts, and social
studies), can be viewed by sections, pages, or even a single picture,

yet be comprehensible and interesting. One illustration within a book
of animals may be clear and relevant to your students, while the illustration next to it may have no relevancy to the group's purpose or
abilities.

Text
Unimportant
There are several ways of using non-fiction with
mentally retarded students. You may teach recogni-
tion of objects, function of objects, relationships
between objects and persons, appreciation of the fine arts and the
practical arts. Obviously there are other uses also! While the non-
fiction text may be useful for acquiring information by the librarian

or teacher who is going to explain or draw attention to the picture, the student must rely solely on that adult's verbal explanation for his/her understanding. The student is not going to read the text to find information. Therefore, whether the text is difficult or easy is unimportant in selecting for non-fiction. That text will have to be adapted by the adult.

Illustrations/ Content

Pictures should clearly illustrate the concept or object being talked about. In non-fiction, illustrations really become a large part of the content. Of course the content should be interesting and within the realm of understanding of your students.

In summary, there are books in both fiction and non-fiction areas that can be appropriately used with mentally handicapped students. Yet, these books are clearly in the minority. To utilize books that may be suitable except for difficulty of text, adaptation of that text to some degree is necessary.

Adult

Arbuthnot, May Hill. The Arbuthnot Anthology of Children's Literature.
New 4th edition revised by Zena Sutherland. New York: Lothrop,
1976.

Includes samples of all types of literature for children:
poems, folktales, fantasy, fables, biography, information. Ideas
for sharing literature with children are also presented.

Bertrand, Penny (Ed.) et al. Books with Options. Boulder, Colorado:
American Association of University Women, 1976.

An annotated booklist designed to help the user find non-
stereotyping books for children. Fiction and non-fiction books
for the primary and elementary child, as well as for the young
adult are listed. Many titles can be adapted for use with the
retarded student. For information write to: Books with Option,
7783 Essex Place, Boulder, Colorado 80301.

Books for Mentally Retarded Children. Cincinnati, Ohio: Public
Library of Cincinnati and Hamilton County, 1973.

A valuable listing of books for mentally retarded children
ages 6 to 15 and trainable children ages 11 to 15. All the titles
were used successfully with one or more classes of retarded
children in the Cincinnati Schools. To order send fifty cents to:
Exceptional Children's Division, Public Library of Cincinnati and
Hamilton County, 800 Vine Street, Cincinnati, Ohio 45203.

Cianciolo, Patricia (Ed.). Picture Books for Children. Chicago:
American Library Association, 1973.

Picture books are grouped under the headings: "Me and My
Family," "Other People," "The World I Live In," and "The Imagina-
tive World." These well-written annotations provide information
about the book's illustrations as well as the story.

31

Johnson, Edna, et al. Anthology of Children's Literature. Boston: Houghton, 1977.

   A collection of outstanding examples from all areas of children's literature including: nursery rhymes, picture books, poetry, folk tales, myths, fiction and biography. A brief annotation introduces each selection and provides valuable insights into the nature of the piece.

Spache, George D. Good Reading for Poor Readers. Champaign, Illinois: Garrard, 1974.

   Because this book contains fiction and non-fiction books arranged according to subject, many of the titles may be appropriately adapted for the intermediate-age child. Of special interest is the inclusion of criteria for selecting books for poor readers.

Yonkers Public Library Children's Services. A Guide to Subjects and Concepts in Picture Book Format. Dobbs Ferry, New York: Oceana Publications, 1979.

   A subject listing of picture books which can be used as a starting point for selection.

Children

(P) - primary child, (I) - intermediate child, (E) - elementary child

Applebaum, Stan. Going My Way? New York: Harcourt Brace Jovanovich, 1976.

   Shows symbiotic relationship among animals, among insects, among flowers. Valuable to explain how one organism is dependent upon another for travel and life. (I)

Barrett, Judi. Peter's Pocket. New York: Atheneum, 1974.

   Interesting book about what can go into pockets. Making pockets activity within the story allows for active participation. (P)

Crews, Donald. _Freight Train_. New York: Greenwillow Books, 1978.

>   Strong lines and bright colors highlight this journey of a freight train. Children may identify the different cars. (P)

Davis, Jane. _Why Does the Tiger Have Stripes?_ Elgin, Illinois: Child's World, 1978.

>   Clearly shows the value of protective coloration of various animals in their everyday environment. Rhyming questions and answers will be readily understood and enjoyed by the handicapped student. (I)

Dickmeyer, Lowell. _Football is For Me_. Minneapolis, MN: Lerner, 1979.

>   The photographs of a team of 11-year-olds in action clearly illustrate how football is played. (I)

Harris, Susan. _Upside-Down Creatures_. New York: Franklin Watts, 1978.

>   An "Easy-Read Wildlife Book," which highlights several creatures which live their lives upside down. Colorful illustrations of the creatures in action add to the book's appeal. (I)

Hoban, Tana. _Shapes and Things_. New York: Macmillan, 1970.

>   Silhouettes of common objects interestingly juxtaposed will stir curiosity. Good participation through guessing of names and shapes. (E)

Lee, Robert J. _The Dinosaur Book_. New York: Golden Press, 1971.

>   A survey of the most popular and fascinating dinosaurs. Ask for distinguishing characteristics of each dinosaur. (I)

Rockwell, Anne. _Toolbox_. New York: Macmillan, 1971.

>   Large, clear illustrations and simple text familiarize students with tools commonly found in their homes. The use of each is explained. (E)

Rockwell, Harlow. _My Doctor_. New York: Macmillan, 1973.

> Informative trip to the doctor's office illustrates simple medical instruments and procedures. Helpful in preparing students for a visit to the doctor. (E)

Swayne, Dick. _I am a Farmer_. Philadelphia: J. P. Lippincott, 1978.

> Color photos show a young girl performing typical farm chores: milking, feeding the animals, and collecting eggs. (P)

Tresselt, Alvin. _Wake Up City_! New York: Lothrop, Lee and Shepard & Co., 1954.

> Good "community helpers" book. Interesting objects to teach and review within each illustration, e.g., find "bus stop." (E)

Turkle, Brinton. _Deep in the Forest_. New York: E. P. Dutton, 1976.

> A reverse-characters story of "Goldilocks" with the little bear exploring the human family's household. A wordless book which lends itself to verbal description and sequencing. (E)

ADAPTING

and TELLING YOUR STORIES

In the preceding chapter on selection, we suggested that there are some fiction books available which can be read to your audience. On the other hand, there are many books which are just too difficult in text to be understood by your students unless some adaptation is made in the telling or reading. This chapter examines methods of adapting such books to make the story more comprehensible for your students.

Preparing a Story

The first step in preparing for a book-sharing time is for you to read the book thoroughly. Dwell on the story awhile before deciding what specific objectives your students should work on for that story.

For the sake of clarification The Alphabet Tale by Jan Garten will be used as an example in this chapter. The Alphabet Tale can be used with both primary and intermediate students.

Intermediate Example

The Alphabet Tale is a "guessing" book in that only the tail of each animal is visible on the right-hand page, and the body of the animal is

seen only by turning to the next page. Thus,
it's a delightful book for both primary and
intermediate students.

Two objectives for an intermediate class
may be the following:

1) Students will name five animals when
   listening to the clues given in the
   rhymes.
2) Students will identify pictures of
   ten animals.

These are not difficult objectives for an
intermediate class of mentally handicapped students, yet they are concrete enough to help you
know why you want to share that book. You may
even estimate that intermediate students will
need a maximum of two session of twenty minutes
each to accomplish these objectives. With such objectives in mind,
there is no need to wonder if what you're doing is beneficial or
important during the lesson. You've thought it well out before story
time!

Primary Example Let's use the same book for a primary class lesson. Are
these objectives appropriate?

1) Students will say the names of five animals when shown the

    pictures.

2) Students will say the name of five animals when viewing only

    the tails of each animal.

These objectives also pinpoint your reasons for using this book

with primary students. Note: it is the same book as above, but you've

recognized that there are different expectations for each of the two

groups.

Changing the Text

Now that we have appropriate objectives that are within grasp of the respective groups, let's look at the adaptation of text necessary for each group.

Intermediate Adaptation

Since one intermediate objective calls for the students to name the animals based on the rhymes, we are assuming that intermediate students are capable of understanding the rhymes with some teaching. Familiarity with the text points out some difficult words--words which must be taught. There are also enough clues within the rhymes to give the students a high probability of correct "guessing" after hearing the rhymes two or three times.

The second objective is even easier to meet. We merely point to an animal and ask the students to name it. Both objectives are within the capabilities of an intermediate class.

In summary, the only "adapting" necessary is an introduction to some words for the purpose of understanding the rhymes!

Primary Adaptation

On the other hand, the primary level group will require more adaptation--but not all that much to be scared off by!

The objectives of the primary students require the students only
to recognize the animals through pictures--pictures of the animals'
bodies and pictures of the animals' tails.

Thus, there is no reason to even say the rhymes to these students.
The rhymes are too difficult to spend time teaching their meanings in
terms of the objectives given here. Yet we would want to introduce them
to the rhyming language of some text just for the pure listening plea-
sure.

The students also "guess" the animals' names by recognizing their
tails. You might merely ask: "Whose tail is this?"

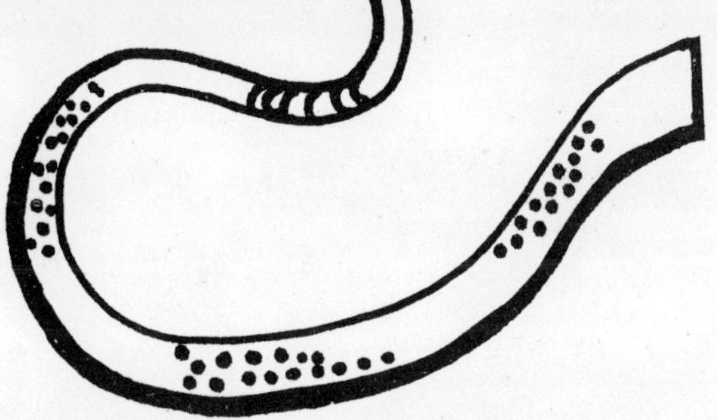

Such a one-liner is understandable and still fun for these younger
students since they guess the animal's name at that point.

For the objective of recognizing the body of the animal, all we
have to do is ask about distinguishing characteristics of that animal,
its name, and perhaps ask for demonstration of the sound it makes. Our
second objective is accomplished.

What we've done here appears obvious--but it's obvious only because we've had the good sense to ask what we wanted to teach from the beginning! Without those objectives, there could have been a hundred mistakes and a hundred wasted minutes!

Successful Story-Sharing Techniques

Telling stories with mentally retarded students is not just a case of "going slower" than you would with average students. That's only a part of it! You're going to have to retell the story in your own words.

Take Little
for Granted
It's better to make sure that your students understand a necessary vocabulary word rather than just assuming that they do. You're going to have to find out what they don't know: they're not going to tell you!

Introduce
the Story
An introduction to a story is always necessary. Try a couple of these openers to get discussion going in desired areas. Who's ever been to the zoo? Find the funniest-looking animal in this book. What animal makes this sound? Take a look at that cage by the door! What's that animal coming in the door?

40

Use Simple Sentences

Obviously you must gear your speaking to the level of your students. For primary students, simple sentences and questions will be appropriate. For intermediate students, your sentence structure should be geared to a greater variety of sentence formations, understandable to your students.

Be Brief

With the mentally handicapped person, it's important to speak briefly before checking on comprehension or allowing verbal interaction. The best way to check on comprehension is to allow time for feedback right after speaking or reading. No long reading of text, or certainly you'll lose them!

Be Enthusiastic

As with any audience, you'll want to be as enthusiastic and bubbly in your presentation as possible. Such enthusiasm is particularly vital to keep your audience's interest from wandering elsewhere.

Guessing

Ahead

Thinking about what comes next is a great passtime for
average students! For our students it's a necessary
part of their curriculum. Thinking ahead, looking and
using clues--are helpful strategies which mentally retarded youngsters
need to develop. When we use this technique with literature, we're
greatly helping that student to develop a practical coping strategy.

To help develop this strategy, ask to which animal the tail in the
picture belongs. In other stories, give time to let students think
about what will happen next. Don't be afraid to remind them of some
past fact which might help with more realistic "guessing."

Check

Comprehension

After every one or two pages of a story, review
the main happenings through questions. Try to
involve as many students as possible in discus-
sion so that you know the main concepts are being understood. If the
story or concepts are not being understood, try simpler questions or
a different strategy.

To help students remember the story, leave a minute or two at the end of the session to review--and relate important sequences and concepts. Without such a review, it'll be that much more difficult for these students to remember the story by the next session.

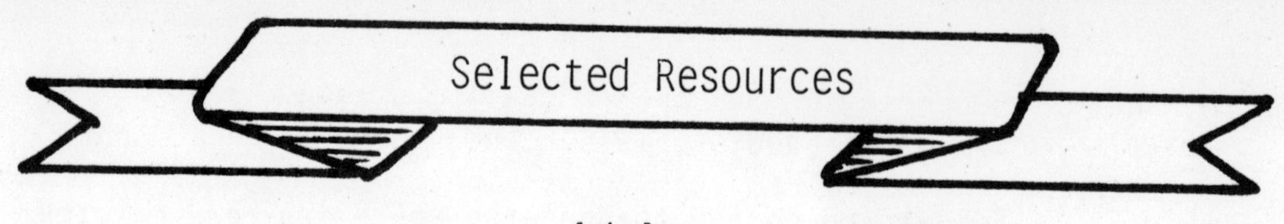

Adult

Bauer, Caroline. <u>Handbook</u> <u>for</u> <u>Storytellers</u>. Chicago: American Library Association, 1977.

All facets of storytelling are covered: planning; promotion; story sources; multimedia storytelling; and programs. An excellent reference when planning storytelling.

Champlin, Connie. <u>Puppetry</u> <u>and</u> <u>Creative</u> <u>Dramatics</u> <u>in</u> <u>Storytelling</u>. Austin, Texas: Nancy Renfro Studios, 1980.

A book for teachers and librarians which incorporates new ways of combining traditional and modern stories with puppetry and creative dramatics.

Cullinan, Bernice E. and Carolyn W. Carmichael. <u>Literature</u> <u>and</u> <u>Young</u> <u>Children</u>. Urbana, Illinois: National Council of Teachers of English, 1977.

A wealth of ideas for sharing literature with children. Many of the books listed in the "100 Best Books and Authors for Young Children" can be adapted for use with the special child.

Greene, Ellin and Madalynne Schoenfeld. <u>Multimedia</u> <u>Approach</u> <u>to</u> <u>Children's</u> <u>Literature</u>. Chicago: American Library Association, 1977.

An annotated list of non-print materials which are book related. Valuable for locating films, filmstrips, and recordings to enhance the students' enjoyment and understanding of literature.

Polette, Nancy. <u>E</u> <u>is</u> <u>for</u> <u>Everybody</u>. Metuchen, NJ: Scarecrow Press, 1976.

Aptly described by the author as a manual for bringing fine picture books into the hands and hearts of children. An annotation and an activity is included for each of the 147 books listed. Ideas and titles can be adapted for use with handicapped students.

Renfro, Nancy. _Puppetry and the Art of Story Creation_. Austin,
    Texas: Nancy Renfro Studios, 1979.

        Exciting new approaches to puppetry which can be used with
    the mentally retarded student include the body puppet and the
    table-top puppet/theater. The development of creativity is
    stressed throughout.

Ross, Ramon R. _Storyteller_. Columbus, Ohio: Charles E. Merrill,
    1972.

        Imaginatively and simply presented, this book includes ideas
    on utilizing songs, puppetry, flannelboard and game exercises to
    enrich storytelling.

Children

(P) - primary child, (I) - intermediate child, (E) - elementary child

Conklin, Gladys. _Little Apes_. New York: Holiday House, 1970.

        Lifelike illustrations of representatives of the four apes
    will appeal to elementary students. (E)

Garten, Jan. _The Alphabet Tale_. New York: Random House, 1964.

        Semi-representational illustrations may create uncertainty
    with some creatures, but overall a valuable book. Students
    participate by guessing animal merely on basis of its tail. Text
    may be used with older students. (E)

Harris, Susan. _Volcanoes_. New York: Franklin Watts, 1979.

        Color photographs and an attractive format make this informa-
    tive book about volcanoes useful with older students. (I)

Koch, Dorothy. _Monkeys are Funny That Way_. New York: Holiday House,
    1962.

        Antics of monkeys will be enjoyed by younger students. (P)

45

Krasilovsky, Phyllis. <u>The</u> <u>Man</u> <u>Who</u> Didn't <u>Wash</u> <u>His</u> <u>Dishes</u>. Garden City,
     New York: Doubleday, 1950.

        The problems a man faces when he doesn't wash his dishes are
     described in this humorous and easily understood story. (E)

Pfloog, Jan. <u>The</u> <u>Zoo</u> <u>Book</u>. New York: Golden Press, 1967.

        Nice "guessing" opportunity by covering part of animal with
     paper and letting students guess what the animal is. Simplify or
     don't use text--merely ask, "This is a ________?" (P)

Ross, Wilda. <u>Can</u> <u>You</u> <u>Find</u> <u>the</u> <u>Animal</u>? New York: Coward, McCann &
     Geoghegan, 1974.

        Students in searching for insects and animals in camouflaged
     environments learn the value of animal/insect protective coloring.
     Making a game of finding the animals in the illustrations will
     increase observational skills. (I)

Selsam, Millicent. <u>Popcorn</u>. New York: William Morrow, 1976.

        Detailed, photographic study of the journey of popcorn from
     seed to plant to popped kernel. (I)

Tresselt, Alvin. <u>The</u> <u>Beaver</u> <u>Pond</u>. New York: Lothrop, Lee and Shepards
     Co., 1970.

        Illustrations by Roger Duvoisin are nearly representational.
     Pictures easily invite interesting comments and questions about
     wildlife. (I)

Ungerer, Tomi. <u>The</u> <u>Three</u> <u>Robbers</u>. Nashville: Atheneum, 1962.

        An unusual mystery involving three robbers who steal an
     orphan. Little text adaptation required. (I)

Urdy, Janice May. <u>A</u> <u>Tree</u> <u>is</u> <u>Nice</u>. New York: Harper, 1956.

        The beauty and usefulness of trees are depicted in this award
     winning picture book. Ask what purpose the tree is serving in
     each picture. (I)

Zaffo, George. <u>Airplanes</u>. New York: Grosset and Dunlap, 1966.

    An adult-appearing book with good opportunities to tell
simple facts about different planes. (I)

GETTING A HANDLE

ON YOUR PUPPET

Merely adapting a book may not be sufficient to allow some mentally handicapped students to understand a particular story. Even when comprehension of the story is not a problem, it's much more fun to include puppets in the study of literature!

Puppets
Help
Learning
Puppets are great to use with handicapped persons for several reasons. The student has an object and a personality to focus upon. He/she senses additional enjoyment in the task, even while it continues to be valuable learning. The puppet becomes an animate "being" who offers the student many positive rewards through its roles as "teacher," "therapist," and "friend."

Since your students will probably be meeting and work-ing with puppets for the first time, it's wise to choose a puppet or puppet material (if you prefer to make one) that will help endear the puppet to your students. Felt, fake fur, socks, knits, and yarns are all warm-feeling materials which make excellent first puppets!

Let's assume that you're going to use a puppet in the library or classroom for general helping activities which pertain to storytelling. Examples of possible activities which your puppet may be responsible for include: greeting the students at storytelling time, praising the students for good behavior, asking students questions

50

pertinent to stories, introducing a book or story, giving book talks,
and assisting you with the actual telling of stories.

It's best to keep one puppet exclusively for such
"general uses" in your library or classroom. Of course,
you'll want to make other puppets
and use them as characters in story telling,
but for now let's concentrate on this "jack-
of-all-trades." Let's refer to this generic
puppet as a "jack puppet" after his many
uses.

Think of personality characteristics for your puppet
which both you and your students would like. Such
characteristics might be handsome or ugly, clever or
foolish, angelic or impish! However, we do want him to be somewhat
respectable in manner and dress since a jack puppet is essentially a
teaching puppet. Yet there is still much room for creativity in his
makeup and personality!

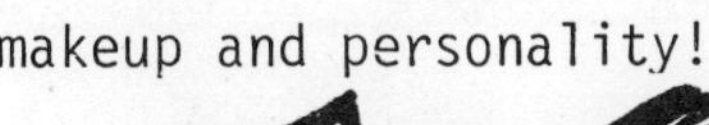

Roles of a Jack Puppet

Give Him a Name   To make it easier to talk about our "general uses" puppet, let's personalize him by giving him a name. Certainly we could call him "Jack," but that's too easy and doesn't really fit the puppet we have in mind. The only name that fits this particular puppet is his real name, "Billy."

Greeter   You may consider any of the following roles for your puppet when working with retarded students. And, of course, you may have additional roles for him in your own class.

Think only in positive terms during story times--before, during, and after! For example, let Billy greet every student as he/she comes into the library or the storytelling circle. Billy may note one special fact about each student, such as, "I like the way you came into the room!", "Don't you have a sharp new haircut!"

Positive Praiser

Try to keep your puppet a positive and humane being. No nasty or negative words should ever leave his lips.

Handicapped students respond admirably to sincere praise, but at the same time they can accept correction given in a positive way. When a student does a good job for him/her, let your puppet say, "Good answer!" and give him/her a hug or handshake!

Gathering the Clan

One common way of announcing your story program is via Billy. He may go around individually to each student and whisper, "Come to the circle for a story," or "I want you to meet Pecos Bill!"

Emcee   At the circle, Billy may call for quiet with dignified

authority or timidly postpone the story until quiet

reigns. Then he may announce the name of the story

before turning the program over to you.

A Keen   Billy may choose

Listener   to sit quietly   and listen

to the story.

When the story ends, he may   comment on the

good manners of the students   and you, in

turn, may ask the students to   evaluate Billy's

listening skills.

Thinking It   Now it's time to think of the specific roles you'd

Through   like your jack puppet to play in the library or

classroom. Write your expectations on paper

similarly to the following chart. Add the activities or actions which

you see your puppet performing to help accomplish the expectations.

Fill in puppet characteristics necessary to fulfill those expectations.

Thinking It Through

Expectations	Characteristics	Activities
reinforces positively	warm, verbal, sincere	-shakes hands with good workers -hugs good workers
ignores inappropriate behavior	warm, shy	-goes away from misbehaving students
announces storytime	verbal, fun-loving	-whispers to students -counts to 5 for quiet
introduces vocabulary	informative, witty, poetic	-pantomimes meaning -uses word in sentence or rhyme
reviews story sequence	inquisitive, forgetful, confused	-asks questions -requests students to pantomime story

Developing Personality

   As with any new-born, your jack puppet's personality will develop
as he grows and matures. You've got to work with him, play with him,
nurture him.

Voice   Now that you have expectations for your puppet, you can
        begin to work on an appropriate voice. Experiment with
        several voices and then narrow the field down to the one
with which you feel most comfortable.

Try various movements, keeping voice and motion suited to each other. Puppets are essentially "action" creatures. Their lives are full of quick, short motions, and these are just as important, if not more so, than any dialogue they may utter.

Practicing movements will help your jack puppet develop a movement repertoire. Put your puppet through the following cadences:

-walk through a cornfield
-trudge up a mountain
-climb a coconut tree
-swim a river
-clap for your efforts

<table>
<tr><td>

**Mirror,
Mirror!**

</td><td>

Use a mirror to practice and you'll see progress whizzing through that glass. When you feel more secure, have a conversation with a neighborhood child. Remember, move-

</td></tr>
</table>

ment comes first!

<table>
<tr><td>

**A Place To
Call . . .**

</td><td>

At home treat the puppet as you wish him to be treated at school . . . as a creature alive and with movement and personality and a voice all his own. Have one

</td></tr>
</table>

place he can call his own . . . an empty shoebox,

a vacant drawer.

Now carry this same regard for your puppet into the library and classroom. Give him a place to sit, to sleep.

When he wakes after a short or long rest, he's certain to be in character!

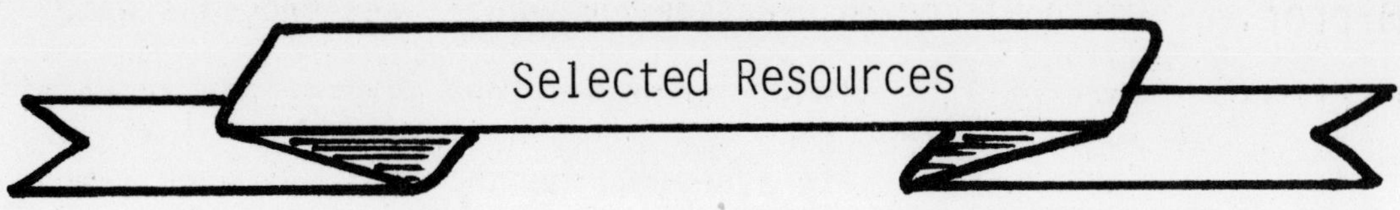

(P) - primary child, (I) - intermediate child, (E) - elementary child

Books

Champlin, Connie. _Puppetry and Creative Dramatics in Storytelling_.
Austin, TX: Nancy Renfro Studios, 1980.

    A lively and clearly written book geared for teachers and
librarians. Built upon a series of "how-to" projects incorporat-
ing new ways to combine traditional and modern children's stories
with simple puppetry and creative dramatics. Includes such aspects
as participation, dialogue, sound effects, action, and pantomime.

Freericks, Mary and Joyce Segal. _Creative Puppetry in the Classroom_.
Rowayton, CT: New Play Books, 1979.

    A good introduction to creating and using puppets effectively.
Ideas discussed include: using a puppet to introduce yourself to
a group; ways of using a mascot puppet; puppets in reading and the
curriculum.

Mangelsen & Sons. _Felt Puppets_. Omaha, NE: Harold Mangelsen and Sons,
n.d.

    Patterns and descriptions for 17 simple mitt-type hand
puppets.

Paludan, Liz. _Playing with Puppets_. New York: Plays, 1975.

    An exciting, brightly illustrated "how-to" book which features
easy-to-make sewn hand puppets. The beginning puppeteer will find
useable ideas on producing puppet plays as well as suggestions for
adapting stories into plays.

Renfro, Nancy. _A Puppet Corner in Every Library_. Austin, TX: Nancy
     Renfro Studios, 1978.

     An excellent idea book for every new puppeteer. Includes
ideas for using puppets in storytelling and as a get-acquainted
friend. Simple puppet patterns are also given.

Sims, Judy. _Puppets for Dreaming and Scheming_. San Francisco: Early
     Stages, 1978.

     A good introduction for anyone interested in educational
puppetry. Ideas for using puppets informally to support curriculum
as well as suggestions for producing simple puppet shows.

Puppet Manufacturers

CLOTH CREATURES--A charming line of furry characters including a croc-o-
     gator, Fuzzy Gnome, Small Furry, dragon, etc. Write to: Cloth
     Creatures, Lynne Jennings, 281 E. Milan Street, Chula Vista, CA
     92010.

NANCY RENFRO STUDIOS--Offers a most unusual and ambitious selection
     including: story time characters to use with books; show person-
     alities for plays; and over 250 characters, including animals,
     insects, people, sea life, holiday, and fairy tale puppets for
     use by children and as loan bag circulation in libraries. Write
     to: Nancy Renfro Studios, 1117 W. 9th Street, Austin, TX 78703.

POSSUM TROT--Makes an extensive line of cuddly, fuzzy animal characters.
     Includes woodland creatures such as bunnies and opossums as well
     as a variety of other animals. Write to: Possum Trot, P. O. Box
     249, McKee, KY 40447.

PUPPET FACTORY--Markets a line of inexpensive, lovable puppet characters
     including a knobby-kneed bird, hippo, turtle, and other imagina-
     tive characters. Write to: Puppet Factory, 160 S. Whisman Road,
     Mountain View, CA 94041.

SELF-EXPRESSION--A resource center of puppet items from a variety of
     manufacturers including R. Dakin & Co., Possum Trot, Sarang Knit
     Puppets, Golden Crown Enterprises, Fisher-Price, and Child Guidance.
     Specializes in educational puppetry. Write to: Self-Expression,
     P. O. Box 65, Mountain Lakes, N.J. 07046.

Organizations

PUPPETEERS OF AMERICA--A national organization for the betterment of
puppetry, with membership from many parts of the world. An
excellent source of information, it offers: an annual Puppet
Festival held at a university in various parts of the country
during summers; the Puppetry Store for purchasing books and puppet
items; a bi-monthly magazine; consultant services in all areas of
puppetry; affiliated guilds located in various regions of the
country. A small annual membership is required. For information
write to: Puppeteers of America, Gayle G. Schuluter, Treasurer,
#5 Cricklewood Path, Pasadena, CA 91107.

PUPPETRY IN EDUCATION--An organization formed in 1977 in response to
the growing interest in puppetry in education. Its purpose is
to serve as a resource center and puppet store while helping to
unite and share ideas among educators in all areas of puppetry
through a bi-monthly newsletter. Membership and newsletter sub-
scription is $10.00 yearly. Write to: PIE NEWS, 164 27th Street,
San Francisco, CA 94110.

PRESENTING

BOOKS WITH PUPPETS

There are many simple ways to use your puppet to help the mentally handicapped student focus on important events, characters, and sequences. This chapter emphasizes the most simple ways--using your puppet to introduce a book and vocabulary, and to check student comprehension.

Fun is Number One! Be sure to be continuously conscious of your overall goal of helping students enjoy literature on their individual levels. Once a story session becomes didactic to the exclusion of the enjoyment of literature, it loses its special awe and magic which storytelling should have at even its most basic level.

Hold Book Your puppet may simply hold the book or help turn pages. The mere fact of seeing even this simple puppet action will gain your students' immediate attention!

Identify
Objects

Having the puppet point to pictures while saying the names of the objects is another way to use your jack puppet simply but effectively. For example, in Virginia Poulet's <u>Blue</u> <u>Bug's</u> <u>Surprise</u>, the puppet may point to each flower, ask the students to repeat the name, and then lead the students in counting the number of flowers on the page. Of course the puppet may also expend praise for good listening, good counting, etc.

Introduce
Vocabulary

This is a fun way to help students look forward to a story while at the same time giving them assistance with vocabulary that will be needed to understand the story.

For example, in Slobodkina's <u>Caps</u> <u>for</u> <u>Sale</u>, the word "peddler" will need some explanation. Let your jack puppet do the following:

-say the word
-have the students repeat the word
-show the picture of the peddler
   trying to sell the caps
-show pictures of modern peddlers
   selling wares on street corners,
   in the home, etc.
-have him whisper words into the
   student's ear

Students Demonstrate   Let the puppet be the peddler who is trying to sell a pencil, a cap, etc., to the students. Have the student say, "Peddler, please sell me a cap!" Change roles and let the student be the peddler. Only by making vocabulary and concepts as functional and meaningful as possible will the retarded student understand and retain these important concepts.

Let's continue with <u>Caps</u> <u>for</u> <u>Sale</u> as our example.
Note how brief an introduction may be while still
being active, to-the-point, and interesting. The
secret to carrying this off is both in puppet actions and your enthusiastic and exaggerated narration.

"Once there was a peddler who sold caps!"
(Puppet holds up his cap or touches student's cap. Teacher or
student puts cap on puppet's head.)

"One day the peddler went to sleep under a great tree."
(Puppet yawns, lays down and sleeps. Student "steals" cap.)

"A terrible thing happened! Some-
body stole the peddler's caps!"
(Puppet awakes and looks everywhere
for the caps.)

"Who do you think stole the peddler's
caps?"
(Puppet lets students individually
whisper their guess into his ear.)

Vary the Introduction

Do the introduction another two or three times, varying your puppet's actions and students' participation. For example, the puppet may look into a student's desk for his caps; a student may hold up his arms, pantomiming the tree.   Such variations and repetitions are just what's needed to help retarded students understand and remember sequence and story plot.

Tell Story Another Day

You may want to introduce the story one day and actually tell it on another day. This is a good idea especially for younger students since it will build enthusiasm while keeping each session fairly short.

Take Your Time

Keep in mind the slowness with which the mentally retarded student learns and the importance for him/her to have different opportunities to hear, say, see, touch, and do. Providing these needed experiences requires much time-- so take that necessary time.

Check
Comprehension

With mentally handicapped youngsters it's vital to continually assess their comprehension of characters, concepts, events, and sequence. This could be a major function of your jack puppet. When a librarian or teacher asks questions over and over, it tends to make the lesson stale and didactic. Let your puppet take turns with you in this function and watch the positive responses from your students.

Check
Comprehension
By Actions

It's also important that your students be checked for understanding through their ability to actually demonstrate difficult concepts.

Let your puppet perform an action and have your students give the
name of the action. Reverse roles and let your students perform the
action while the puppet responds with praise or needed correction.

Puppet
Makes
Mistake   A fun alternative is to have your puppet demonstrate the
action incorrectly, and then let your students determine
if it was done correctly or incorrectly. Have the students show your puppet the correct way!

For example, you might check student comprehension of "peddler
selling" by having your jack puppet perform the batting behavior of a
baseball player (or the swimming motions of a swimmer). If no squeals
of "wrong!" come from your students, you wonder aloud whether that
motion was really that of a "peddler selling."

Ask your students to show your puppet how a peddler really sells!

Repetitive Phrases

Puppets are wonderful leaders and assistants for cuing students. Just a first word or two of a repetitive phrase will start your students on their rhyming way.

In <u>Alphabet Tale</u> by Jan Garten, students might try giving the name of the animal by viewing only its tail. Your jack puppet may help by cuing at the appropriate time with, "It's a . . . !" Watch your students take off!

Reading A Story

For a very short narrative, your puppet may want to read the whole story. Such an invitation should come from you, rather than the students, since you are the person in control.

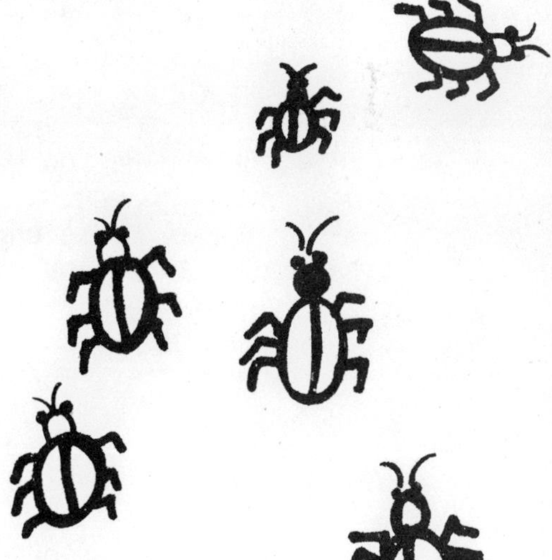

If you do use your jack puppet for such reading, make the story short and lively. Examine the <u>Blue Bug</u> series by Virginia Poulet and

71

you'll see these stories with minimal word content text as very appropriate for this use.

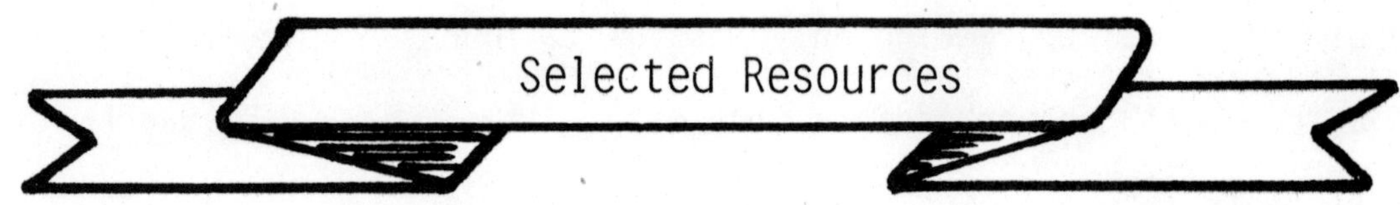

Selected Resources

(P) - primary child, (I) - intermediate child, (E) - elementary child

General

Barton, Byron. <u>Buzz</u>, <u>Buzz</u>, <u>Buzz</u>. New York: Macmillan, 1973.

    A bee stinging a bull is the beginning of a chain reaction
which has many amusing incidents. Characters include a cow, goat,
mule, farmer, and the farmer's wife. Cover the words and let the
puppet encourage the children to retell the story from the pictures. (I)

Carle, Eric. <u>Do</u> <u>You</u> <u>Want</u> <u>to</u> <u>be</u> <u>My</u> <u>Friend</u>? New York: Crowell, 1971.

    A mouse encounters a variety of animal tails and asks, "Do
you want to be my friend?" The complete animal is met on the
following page and none wants to be mouse's friend until another
mouse appears on the last page. Similar to <u>The</u> <u>Alphabet</u> <u>Tale</u> by
Jan Garten. (E)

Garten, Jan. <u>The</u> <u>Alphabet</u> <u>Tale</u>. New York: Random House, 1964.

    Semi-representational illustrations may create uncertainty
with some creatures, but overall a valuable book. Students must
participate by guessing animal merely on basis of its tail. Text
may be used with older students. Similar to Eric Carle's <u>Do</u> <u>You</u>
<u>Want</u> <u>to</u> <u>be</u> <u>My</u> <u>Friend</u>? (E)

Goins, Ellen. <u>David's</u> <u>Pockets</u>. Austin, TX: Steck-Vaughn Co., 1972.

       Forest objects are nicely illustrated while at the same time giving an incentive for your students to go on a "treasure hunt." Recommended for primary only because very young boy is central character. (P)

Keats, Ezra Jack. <u>Pssst!</u> <u>Doggie</u>. New York: Franklin Watts, Inc., 1973.

       A wordless book of a dancing cat and dog provides opportunities to develop humor as well as spatial concepts (around, up, etc.) (P)

Livermore, Elaine. <u>Three</u> <u>Little</u> <u>Kittens</u> <u>Lost</u> <u>Their</u> <u>Mittens</u>. Boston: Houghton, 1979.

       In this modern adaptation of the popular rhyme, the kittens lose their mittens in a variety of interesting places, i.e., the library, candy store, the snow. The puppet can help locate the hidden mitten on each page. (P)

Maestro, Betsy and Givlio. <u>Where</u> <u>is</u> <u>My</u> <u>Friend?</u> New York: Crown Publishers, Inc., 1976.

       Basic spatial concepts of "up, down, between, around, etc." clearly illustrated on double-spread pages. Children can use puppet to show understanding of concepts. (P)

Poulet, Virginia. <u>Blue</u> <u>Bug's</u> <u>Surprise</u>. Chicago: Childrens Press, 1977.

       Good illustrations and minimal text allow for a variety of activities in counting and naming objects. Other titles in <u>Blue</u> <u>Bug</u> series also excellent for teaching basic concepts. (P)

Parish, Peggy. <u>Dinosaur</u> <u>Time</u>. New York: Harper and Row, 1974.

       Most students will enjoy the strange creatures. Having the students describe the dinosaurs will help their verbal skills. Older students will want to listen to the simple but excellent text descriptions. (E)

73

    The following are grouped by animal puppets which could be used to introduce the story.

Bear Puppet

Freeman, Don. _Corduroy_. New York: Viking Press, 1968.

> A warm story about a little girl, a department store teddy bear, and a lost button. Appropriate for younger children since main character is a young child. (P)

Gretz, Susanna. _Teddy Bears ABC_. New York: Follett, 1975.

> A group of teddy bears and their animal friends have many adventures as they travel from A to Z. Will teach and reinforce alphabet skills. (P)

Holl, Adelaide. _Bedtime for Bears_. New York: Garrard, 1973.

> A little bear learns that winter time is for sleeping. Good motivation for discussion of habits of bears. (P)

Dog Puppet

Bemelmans, Ludwig. _Madeline's Rescue_. New York: Viking, 1953.

> A dog saves two young French girls from drowning and is taken to live in their boarding school only to learn that dogs cannot live at the school. (I)

Binzen, Bill. _Rory Story_. Garden City, N.Y.: Doubleday, 1974.

> A photo story depicting the growth of a playful golden retriever from puppy to full grown dog. Will be of interest to students with dogs as pets. (P)

Domanska, Janina. _Spring Is_. New York: Greenwillow Books, 1976.

> The seasons of the year are discovered by a frisky dachshund. Can be followed by a discussion of characteristics of each season or activities appropriate for each season. (P)

Mayer, Mercer. <u>Boy, a Dog, and a Frog</u>. New York: Dial Press, 1967.

       A wordless book describing the unsuccessful efforts of a
boy and his dog to catch a frog. Students can tell story in
their own words. (E)

Zion, Gene. <u>Harry, the Dirty Dog</u>. New York: Harper & Row, 1956.

       Harry, a white dog with black spots, runs away from home
rather than take a bath. His adventures make Harry so dirty that
no one recognizes him when he returns home until he takes a bath!
(E)

Monkey Puppet

Goodall, John S. <u>Jacko</u>. New York: Harcourt Brace Jovanovich, 1971.

       The adventures of an organ grinders monkey who escapes and
returns to his jungle home are told with no words but delightful
illustrations. Older students will enjoy telling this story. (I)

Slobodkina, Esphyr. <u>Caps for Sale</u>. Reading, Mass.: Addison Wesley,
    1947.

       Humorous tale of how a peddler outwits monkeys who have
taken his caps. Always a hit. (E)

Snake Puppet

Carle, Eric. <u>The Very Hungry Caterpillar</u>. Cleveland, Ohio: Collins-
    World, 1970.

       A caterpillar on its way to becoming a butterfly eats so
many unusual things that it gets a stomach ache. Students can
name and count objects. (P)

Lionni, Leo. <u>Inch by Inch</u>. New York: I. Obolensky, 1960.

>A clever inch worm uses its natural abilities to outsmart a bird. (P)

Ungerer, Tomi. <u>Crictor</u>. New York: Harper, 1958.

>An amusing story of an old lady who has a boa constrictor as a pet. Older students will enjoy this story's humor. (I)

CHORAL SPEAKING

WITH PUPPETS

Many traditional stories in children's literature utilize repetitive phrases to excellent advantage. Think of the delightful tales from which the following come.

"Who's that tripping over my bridge?"
"Then I'll huff and I'll puff, and I'll blow your
   house in."
"Oh! We're going to tell the king the sky's a-falling."
"Cats here, cats there, cats and kittens everywhere.
   Hundreds of cats, . . ."

The first three are traditional folk tales: "The Three Billy
Goats Gruff," "The Three Little Pigs," and "Henny-Penny" or "Chicken-
Little." The last is a modern tale (1928), <u>Millions</u> <u>of</u> <u>Cats</u>, which
recognizes the vitality of repetitive phrases in children's litera-
ture.

Advantages
of Choral
Speaking

For mentally retarded children there is the important
plus of creating positive group feeling while building self-concept in choral speaking. By adding
simple puppets, student comprehension will also increase. Even though
we're still at a relatively simple level of participation, every student is doing three important mental exercises: memorizing a choral

line to some degree, saying the line at the appropriate literary point,

and demonstrating understanding of the story by means of a puppet.

Our main goal of having our students speak in choral parts is to increase fun and understanding. Therefore, we shouldn't care about the usual elementary school goal of teaching students to speak in perfect unison.

For one thing, speaking in unison is an extremely difficult matter to teach average and above-average students. Secondly, great emphasis is placed on unison speaking because a performance before an audience is expected. Such is not the case with mentally handicapped youngsters. If our students are able to learn their parts so that they remember the main words, that is sufficient. If they start off together but end up at different times, that's also adequate.

| Larger Group | For the librarian and teacher, there is a pleasant advantage in choral speaking of being able to concentrate on one larger group doing the same learning--no different |

parts to teach, no different puppets to make. Everything is simple and standard--except the students' learning rates of course! This difference in rate of learning can be handled by briefly tutoring small groups according to their difficulty with a specific choral part.

| Student/ Librarian Roles | Your role in choral speaking with puppets is to narrate the story and provide the necessary cues and coordination for the students to carry through their |

choral parts. The students will have to learn their choral parts as well as coordinate their use of simple puppets.

| Introduce Vocabulary | Let's use the story, "The Gingerbread Boy" as our example for teaching choral parts. One essential vocabulary word to teach here is "gingerbread." |

Unless the students actually taste gingerbread cookie or cake, they will have no idea of

its very different tangy taste. So bring in some cookies or cake and
let the students talk about its taste.

**Change
Vocabulary**
Other foods unknown to our students are also part of
the story--cinnamon and currants. We'd recommend
substituting known foods, rather than teach such
relatively uncommon foods. For example, peanuts can replace cinnamon
seeds for the jacket buttons, and raisins can replace currants for the
boy's eyes. Such adaptation of text can save a lot of unnecessary
teaching of unimportant and non-functional words.

<table>
<tr><td>Read
Story</td><td>Read the picture book. Be sure students understand the story. Stress the choral sections. Read the story a couple of times while encouraging students to join the</td></tr>
</table>

choral sections.

In the "Gingerbread Boy," emphasize the phrase:

"Run, run! as fast as you can.
You can't catch me, I'm the Gingerbread Man."

Again, don't worry about teaching the phrase completely to every student, and don't spend more than five to ten minutes for a couple of days practicing the chorus.

Dividing
Parts

There are two basic ways of dividing lines for teaching. The usual is simply to teach the lines as the student would normally say them in sequence.

For example, you'd first teach "Run, run! as fast as you can." When the student has that part memorized, then you'd teach "You can't catch me, I'm the Gingerbread Man." In technical terminology, this is "forward chaining."

Backward
Chaining

Often mentally handicapped students memorize more easily when you begin teaching the last section first. For example, you'd teach "You can't catch me, I'm the Gingerbread Man." first. When this is learned sufficiently, then teach the preceding line, "Run, run! as fast as you can." The advantage to backward chaining is that the student continues saying the lines already memorized after each attempt at memorizing the preceding line.

Example: Visualize a student learning the following. Here the last line has already been learned and the preceding line is only now being taught.

Student: "Run . . . fast. . . ."

"You can't catch me, I'm the Gingerbread Man."

This method assures that the student will not forget previously
learned lines since he/she continues to say them even as he practices
his new lines.

Making Simple Paper Bag Puppets

Puppets will help the students become more a part of the lesson,
and will help you determine how much of the story the student is actually
understanding. You can do this by observing the student in his/her
use of the puppet, as well as by asking questions of the puppet. For
example in "Gingerbread Boy," you might ask a puppet: "Who was just
chasing you?" or "Why are you running away?"

Paper Bag   A brown lunch-size paper bag can be made quickly into

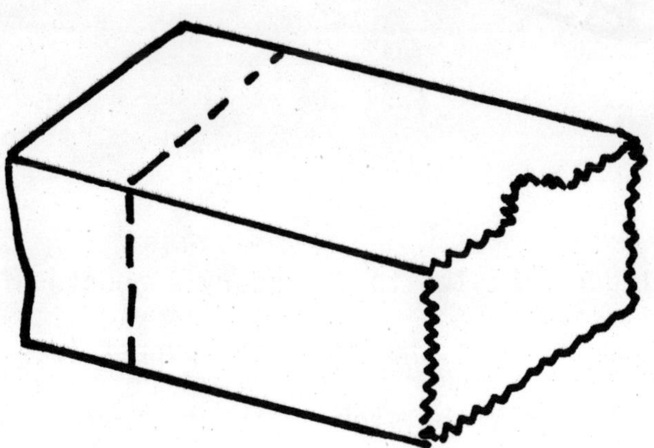

a character puppet by
your students. Students
can make this puppet in
one sitting though
you'll have to give
direction and reassurance
the first time through
with this type of puppet.

The following will enable beginners to make a quick
paper bag puppet.

-lunch-size paper bag
-masking tape
-glue
-scissors
-crayons
-construction paper
-cloth and yarn bits

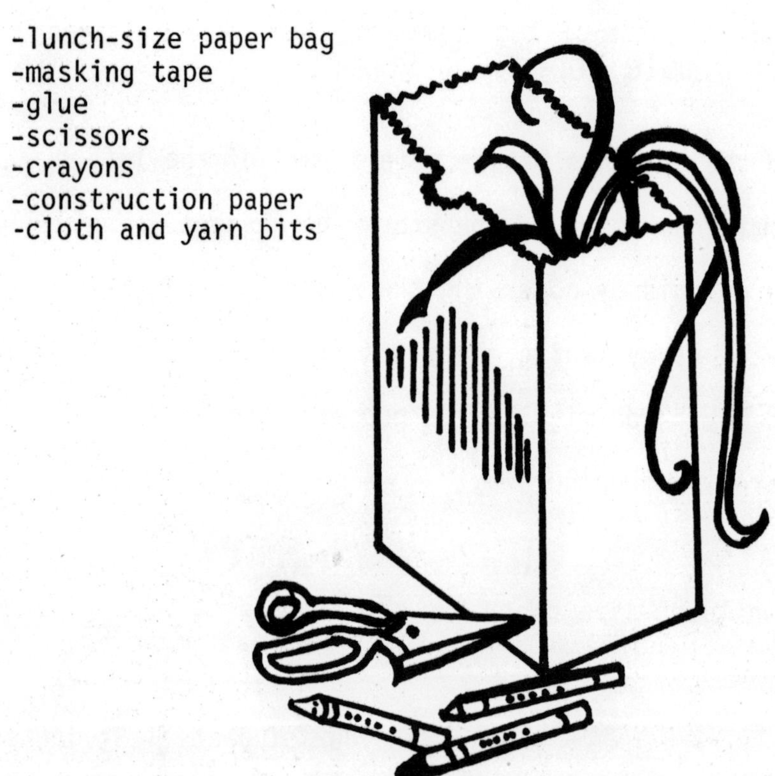

Have the students listen to the story a couple of times.
When it's time to make the character puppet (e.g., "Gingerbread Boy"), tell the story without showing the pictures. This will help the students create a more original puppet.

Show them a paper bag puppet of another character, since mentally
handicapped youngsters need to see the finished product they're working
toward.

a)   Ask students to think of the shape they want their "Ginger-
     bread Boy" to be. Have them tell you or the jack puppet
     the shape they've chosen for his face.

b)   Have the students outline the face in crayon on the bag,
     making sure that the
     side of the bag with
     the fold is being
     drawn upon. Students
     may use this fold as
     the mouth, top of the
     head, or a hat.

c)   Use crayon to outline
     and color in facial
     features of character.
     More difficult to do
     is accenting of facial
     features with colored
     paper and cloth bits.

d)   Students may want to make a body for the "Gingerbread Boy"
with his characteristic feature of buttons, or not-so-
characteristic features of gaily-colored pants, etc.

Sequencing Stories--A Variation   Another type of story in which choral parts may be effectively used with our students is that of the sequence story. For example, in the story of <u>Drummer Hoff</u>, each soldier who is introduced is done so by the choral line.

Have your students make puppets to represent the various characters
of the story. By keeping these in the classroom, you'll soon increase

your repertoire of stories suitable for telling in choral speaking/paper
bag puppet style. Also, note some of the titles in "Selected Resources"
and you'll see that more stories for telling older students becomes
readily possible.

Tips for Increasing Esteem

Now that your students are feeling more and more like performers, you may want to have them "tell a story" to a first or second grade class, or to the principal.
However, caution yourself that this is not meant to be a performance for
an audience (with all the implications of perfection, formality, etc.),
but rather as a means of building your students' esteem.

Another way to increase importance and participation of your students in storytelling is to videotape their story. In reviewing the
story, the students will certainly be able to tell you what they did

really well. In any case, it is bound to emphasize the importance of their efforts in storytelling.

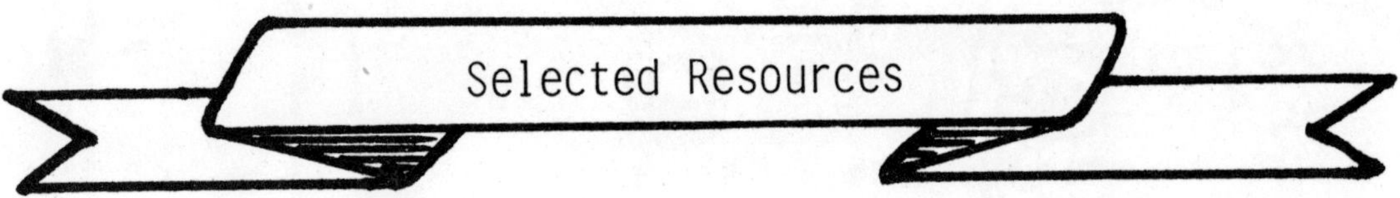

Selected Resources

(P) - primary child, (I) - intermediate child, (E) - elementary child

Carle, Eric. <u>Have You Seen My Cat</u>? New York: Franklin Watts, 1976.

> As a boy searches for his missing cat, he encounters a variety of cats; jaguar, tiger, lion, cheetah. . . . Children can ask, "Have you seen my cat?" Children answer, "This is not my cat." (P)

Emberley, Barbara. <u>Drummer Hoff</u>. Englewood Cliffs, N.J.: Prentice-Hall, 1967.

> A delightful tale, told in repetitive verse, of the building and firing of a cannon. Bold woodcuts add to the appeal of this book. Children will enjoy joining in on the refrain, "Drummer Hoff fired it off." (I)

Gag, Wanda. <u>Millions of Cats</u>. New York: Coward, McCann & Geoghegan, 1928.

> A childless couple wants a cat but almost get more than they can handle. A repetitive chant adds to the fun of this story. ("Hundreds of cats, thousands of cats, millions and billions and trillions of cats.") (E)

Galdone, Paul. <u>The</u> <u>Little</u> <u>Red</u> <u>Hen</u>. New York: Seabury, 1973.

      Friends of the Little Red Hen are all eager to help her eat
the bread she's baked even if they didn't want to help with the
work. ("Not I.") Paul Galdone has also illustrated versions of
<u>Henny</u> <u>Penny</u> ("The Sky is falling") and The <u>Gingerbread</u> <u>Boy</u> ("Run,
run as fast as you can. . . .") which are suitable for choral
speaking. (E)

Holdsworth, William Curtis. <u>The</u> <u>Gingerbread</u> <u>Boy</u>. New York: Farrar,
    Straus & Girous, 1968.

      The illustrations in this version show the sequential length-
ening of the characters trying to catch the gingerbread boy. Thus,
this version is especially good for the retarded child. ("Run,
run as fast as you can. You can't catch me I'm the Gingerbread
Man.") (E)

Hutchins, Pat. <u>Goodnight</u> <u>Owl</u>. New York: Macmillan, 1972.

      During the day when Owl tries to sleep, all the other
creatures that live in his tree are making their usual sounds.
While they try to sleep at night, Owl takes his turn making noise.
Children can participate by making the sounds of each animal. (P)

Kellogg, Steve. <u>There</u> <u>Was</u> <u>an</u> <u>Old</u> <u>Woman</u>. New York: Parents' Magazine
    Press, 1974.

      The tragic story of an old woman with a most unusual
appetite who swallowed a fly, spider, bird, cat, dog, cow. She
died trying to swallow a horse, of course. ("I don't know why
she swallowed the fly, perhaps she'll die.") (E)

Preston, Edna Mitchell. <u>One</u> <u>Dark</u> <u>Night</u>. New York: Viking, 1969.

      This simple tale involves a group of Halloween characters
who are frightened by a scary noise one dark night. The surprise
ending always delights listeners. Similar in style to "The
House That Jack Built." ("One dark night.") (E)

Quackenbush, Robert. <u>Old</u> <u>MacDonald</u> <u>Had</u> <u>a</u> <u>Farm</u>. New York: Lippincott,
    1972.

        Strong, colorful illustrations take the reader for a humorous
    visit to Old MacDonald's farm. ("With a _____ _____ here, and a
    _____ _____ there. . . .") (E)

Seuling, Barbara. <u>The</u> <u>Teeny</u> <u>Tiny</u> <u>Woman</u>. New York: Viking Books, 1976.

        A ghost story about a teeny tiny woman who finds a teeny
    tiny bone in a graveyard. When the owner of the bone asks for it
    back, the teeny tiny woman gives a surprising answer. Children
    can use spooky voices as they recite the refrain, "Give me my
    bone." (I)

Sivulich, Sandra. <u>I'm</u> <u>Going</u> <u>on</u> <u>a</u> <u>Bear</u> <u>Hunt</u>. New York: G. P. Dutton,
    1973.

        As a boy goes on a bear hunt children can join in by per-
    forming the actions and repeating parts of the verse. Good intro-
    duction to making sounds, actions, and remembering sequence. A
    fun exercise for all ages. (E)

RHYMES and VERSES

WITH PUPPETS

Rhymes and poems have always been a delight to children. They can be made meaningful to the retarded child as well--with the help of puppets! While average students easily understand traditional and modern rhymes, retarded students have a difficult time unless librarians and teachers make them meaningful through explanation, demonstration--and puppets!

Three Puppet Types

This chapter examines the three types of puppets which can aid comprehension of this literary genre.

"Paper plate" puppets have been selected for their ease in manufacture by students and adults, along with the simple motoric skills needed for operating them.

<table>
<tr><td>

Selecting

Rhymes

</td><td>

Rhymes, of course, are already set in stone--there
is no valid way in which they can be changed to
increase understanding, unlike narrative stories in

</td></tr>
</table>

which vocabulary may be easily substituted. Once a word is changed in

a rhyme, the rhyme ceases to be or loses its effectiveness.

Selection Factors for Rhymes and Poems

<table>
<tr><td>

Simple

Is Best

</td><td>

Traditional rhymes usually have one character who is the
protagonist throughout. The "Mother Goose Nursery
Rhymes" exemplify such one-character rhymes (e.g., "Mary,

</td></tr>
</table>

Mary quite contrary," and "Little Jack Horner").

<table>
<tr><td>

**Complex
Is Out**

</td><td>

The more modern nonsense rhymes (late 19th and 20th cen-
turies) are more complex and more dependent on unorthodox
use of language which the retarded student will undoubt-

</td></tr>
</table>

edly experience great difficulty. Examples of poets of nonsense verses
include Edward Lear and Ogden Nash.

<table>
<tr><td>

Vocabulary

</td><td>

Since rhymes are generally historical and traditional,
some words will not be familiar to your students.
Therefore, it's necessary to give only sufficient

</td></tr>
</table>

explanation for the rhyme to be understood and made delightful. The
student is probably never going to use that new vocabulary word in
everyday language, so spend minimal time teaching--only enough for that
word to be understood in the context of the specific rhyme.

<table>
<tr><td>

**Age
Appropriate**

</td><td>

Verse, as a part of children's literature, is a
particularly sensitive area which librarians and
teachers need to be aware when working with the

</td></tr>
</table>

retarded student. Unlike picture books, this genre is usually designated only for preschool and early primary grades. Additionally,
rhymes are also usually memorized and said outside of school as well
as in school.

Since older retarded students in social situations should be act-
ing as much as possible like their average age-mates, we should be
careful about using certain nursery rhymes with intermediate and older
students.

A few rhymes whose content is appropriate for the intermediate retarded student include: "Tom, Tom, the Piper's Son," "There was a Crooked Man," and "This is the House That Jack Built." When selecting rhymes for this age group, be sure that a small child is not the main character nor that infantile themes dominate.

Making One-Sided Paper Plate Puppets

Single Character Rhymes   This type of puppet is especially useful when there is only one character who maintains a single mood throughout. Many variations are available in using this puppet: all students make the same puppet; each student makes a different puppet representing a different rhyme; each student learns his/her specific rhyme; all students learn all rhymes.

Student Role   The student merely holds the puppet full-faced toward the audience and moves the puppet in rhythm with the words of the rhyme. Narration may be done by adult or students.

Examples   Examples of rhymes and chants which work well with this type of puppet follow:

<u>Lady Bug</u>

Lady Bug, Lady Bug,
    Fly away.
You're house is on fire,
    And you're children
        will burn.

A <u>Bear</u> <u>Went</u> <u>Over</u> <u>the</u> <u>Mountain</u>

A bear went over the mountain,
A bear went over the mountain,
A bear went over the mountain,
To see what he could see!

The other side of the mountain,
The other side of the mountain,
The other side of the mountain,
Was all that he could see.

There <u>Was</u> <u>an</u> <u>Old</u> <u>Woman</u>

There was an old woman
Lived under the hill,
And if she's not gone
She lives there still.

Fee, <u>Fi</u>, <u>Fo</u>, <u>Fum</u>

Fee, fi, fo, fum,
    I smell the blood of an Englishman:
Be he alive or be he dead,
    I'll grind his bones to make my bread.

<u>Little Boy Blue</u>

Little Boy Blue,
    Come blow your horn,
The sheep's in the meadow,
    The cow's in the corn!

Where is the boy
    Who looks after the sheep?
He's under a haycock
    Fast asleep.

Will you wake him?
    No, not I,
For if I do,
    He's sure to cry.

<u>Jack be Nimble</u>

Jack be nimble,
    Jack be quick,
Jack jump over
    The candlestick.

Materials
Needed

To make this puppet (e.g., Jack in "Jack be Nimble,")

you'll need the following:

-an 8" or 10" paper plate
-crayons
-bits of cloth scraps
-dowel or tongue depressor
-masking tape
-magic markers

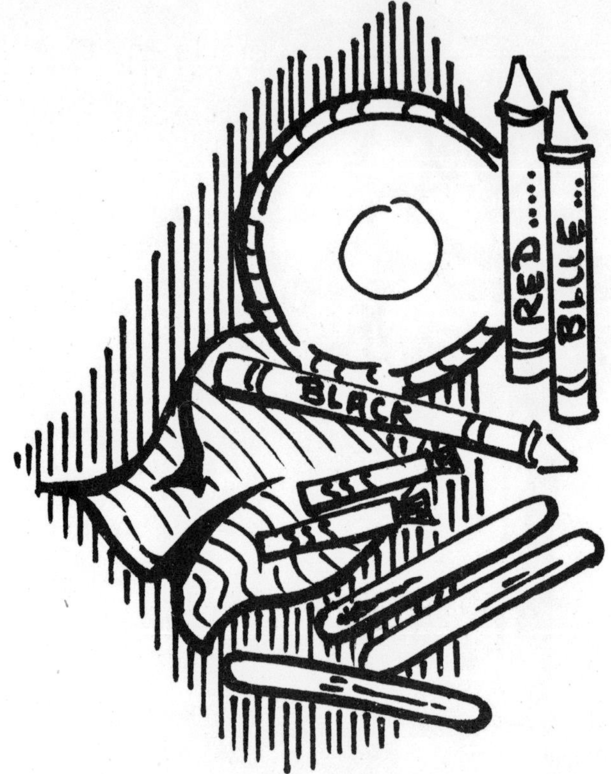

Students
Can Make

If students are going to make this puppet, "Jack," have them first listen to the rhyme and imagine what Jack looks like. You're likely to have greater student creativity by not showing them a puppet of "Jack," but rather a puppet character from another rhyme or story.

Group
Process

Begin by showing the students the type of puppet they're going to make, that is, a paper plate puppet. Take the group through the following process:

a)   Use crayons to make Jack's hair and facial features

b)   Color facial features, outline the outer edge of the plate with

        a dark color or add bits of yarn and felt to Jack's hair, eye-

        brows, and lips.

c)   Use masking tape to attach a dowel piece or tongue depressor to

        the back of the plate. Be sure it's lined up correctly to serve

        as the puppet's "handle."

Making Two-Sided Paper Plate Puppets

Character   This puppet expands on the preceding in that both

Changes   sides of the plate (or two attached plates) are used

Mood   to make different views of the same character, For

example, the character in the rhyme, "There was a Little Girl, Who Had

101

a Little Curl," has two distinct sides to her nature--a "very, very
good" side and a "horrid" side.

To work this puppet, the student begins with the appropriate side and then turns to the other side of the
character when the narration calls for it.

In addition to the materials used in making the "one-
sided paper plate" puppet above, you also need a
second paper plate and a stapler.

-two 8" or 10" paper plates
-stapler
-crayons
-bits of cloth scraps

-dowel or tongue depressor
-masking tape
-magic markers

Use the same general procedure as with the "one-sided
paper plate" puppet. The difference is that you'll
be using one plate for each of the character's different expressive moods.

When each view is completed, position the plates in correct upright positions, so that a mere twist of the "handle" would make both faces appear upright. Tape the tongue depressor or the dowel to the back of one plate. Now staple the rim of the two plates together at three or four evenly-spaced spots. Also staple the plates on either side of the "handle" for extra strength.

Examples   Listed are samples of rhymes with different character changes that work well with "two-sided paper plate" puppets.

Humpty Dumpty

Humpty Dumpty sat on a wall,
Humpty Dumpty had a great fall;
All the King's horses and all the
      king's men
Couldn't put Humpty together again.

<u>There Was a Little Girl</u>

There was a little girl
Who had a little curl,
Right in the middle of her forehead.
When she was good,
She was very, very good.
But when she was bad, she was horrid!

<u>Polly Put the Kettle On</u>

Polly put the kettle on,
Polly put the kettle on,
Polly put the kettle on,
We'll all have tea.

Sukey take it off again,
Sukey take it off again,
Sukey take it off again,
They're all gone away.

<u>Jack</u> <u>Sprat</u>

Jack Sprat could eat no fat,
   His wife could eat no lean,
And so between them both, you see,
   They licked the platter clean.

Making Box-Stage Puppets

Characters Come and Go

This puppet mode is very useful when there are characters who appear and disappear during the story or rhyme. For example, in "Little Miss Muffet," the little girl appears alone on stage initially. The spider then comes on stage to frighten Miss Muffet who then goes off stage with a fright.

Character On- Character Off	Begin with the puppets invisible within the box or cup. As the rhyme or story unfolds and the character is mentioned, push the appropriate straw up

so that the character can be seen by the "audience." Keep the onstage

character(s) active with small movements of the straw or handle.

Characters appear or disappear from stage according to the narration

of the rhyme or story.

Materials Needed	Materials for this puppet include the following.

-paper cups, cereal boxes with tops removed
-thin cardboard or oaktag
-drinking straws (paper)
-masking tape
-crayons
-magic markers
-scissors

This type of puppet has a wide variety of basic materials which can be used in the basic structure. For example the basic "stage" may be a paper cup, a paper paint bucket, a cereal box (rectangular) or an oatmeal box (round).

The box or cup serves as the basic "stage" while the puppets are made of thin cardboard attached to a straw or thin stick. The straw is then placed into the box or cup by cutting a tight hole in the box or cup bottom. When a character comes "onstage," the student simply pushes up the correct straw from beneath the box or cup. The student holds the box or cup in one hand and operates the puppets with the other.

First select an appropriate-sized cup/box which is
adequate in "stage area" to contain the necessary
number of puppets included in the rhyme. Three puppets
is the maximum which students can appropriately maneuver.

Cut out your characters full-body from the thin cardboard or oaktag. Use crayons and markers for features and outlining of body.

Attach the back of the puppets
to straws with masking tape. Having
considered the stage position for
each puppet, pierce a small hole
barely large enough for the straw
to be pushed up and down.

There is a great number of rhymes that fit nicely into this mode. The more popular ones include: "Jack and Jill," "Little Miss Muffet," "Hickory, Dickory, Dock," "Humpty Dumpty," "Ding Dong Bell," and "Old Mother Hubbard."

<u>Little</u> <u>Miss</u> <u>Muffet</u>

Little Miss Muffet
Sat on a tuffet,
Eating her curds and whey;
There came a big spider,
Who sat down beside her
And frightened Miss Muffet away.

<u>Itsy</u>, <u>Bitsy</u>, <u>Spider</u>

Itsy, bitsy spider went up the water spout.
Down came the rain, and washed the spider out.
Out came the sun and dried up all the rain.
Itsy, bitsy spider went up the spout again.

<u>Mary's Lamb</u>

Mary had a little lamb,
Its fleece was white as snow;
And everywhere that Mary went
The lamb was sure to go.

He followed her to school one day;
That was against the rule;
It made the children laugh and play
To see a lamb at school.

<u>This</u> <u>is</u> <u>the</u> <u>Way</u> <u>the</u> <u>Ladies</u> <u>Ride</u>

This is the way the ladies ride,
    Nim, nim, nim, nim.
This is the way the gentlemen ride,
    Trim, trim, trim, trim.
This is the way the farmers ride,
    Trot, trot, trot, trot.
This is the way the huntsmen ride,
    A-gallop, a-gallop, a-gallop, a-gallop.

(P) - primary child, (I) - intermediate child, (E) - elementary child

Briggs, Raymond. <u>The</u> <u>Mother</u> <u>Goose</u> <u>Treasury</u>. New York: Coward-McCann,
    1966.

    A collection of over 400 rhymes, each illustrated, which can
serve as a resource since it includes the most popular rhymes as
well as many rhymes which are less familiar. (E)

111

Galdone, Paul. <u>The</u> <u>History</u> <u>of</u> <u>Simple</u> <u>Simon</u>. New York: McGraw Hill,
     1966.

     The adventures of Simple Simon are humorously depicted in
this picture book. (P)

Galdone, Paul. <u>House</u> <u>That</u> <u>Jack</u> <u>Built</u>. New York: McGraw Hill, 1961.

     Droll illustrations highlight this popular repetitive
rhyme. (E)

Glazer, Tom. <u>Do</u> <u>Your</u> <u>Ears</u> <u>Hang</u> <u>Low?</u> Garden City, New York: Doubleday,
     1980.

     Fifty musical finger plays with clear directions, piano
arrangements, and guitar chords. Includes "Little Bo-Peep,"
"Little Jack Horner," and "Over in the Meadow." <u>Eye</u> <u>Winker</u>
<u>Tom</u> <u>Tinker</u> <u>Chin</u> <u>Chopper</u> (1973) by the same author includes 50
different musical fingerplays. (E)

Ness, Evaline. <u>Old</u> <u>Mother</u> <u>Hubbard</u> <u>and</u> <u>Her</u> <u>Dog</u>. New York: Holt,
     Rinehardt and Winston, 1972.

     A comical Mother Hubbard and her sheep dog make this single
edition of the Mother Goose rhyme popular with students of all
ages. (E)

Petersham, Maud and Miska. <u>The</u> <u>Rooster</u> <u>Crows</u>. New York: MacMillan,
     1945.

     A collection of American rhymes and jingles whose humor will
appeal to older students. (I)

Reed, Philip. <u>Mother</u> <u>Goose</u> <u>and</u> <u>Nursery</u> <u>Rhymes</u>. New York: Atheneum,
     1963.

     The colorful woodcuts and thoughtful use of space make this
a particularly appealing version of Mother Goose rhymes. (P)

Tashjian, Virginia A., Comp. <u>Juba</u> <u>This</u> <u>and</u> <u>Juba</u> <u>That</u>. Boston: Little,
     Brown, 1969.

          A collection of rhymes, chants, riddles, stories, and songs
     which invite participation. The finger play section includes "I'm
     a Little Teapot" and "Eensy Weensy Spider." (I)

Wildsmith, Brian. <u>Brian</u> <u>Wildsmith's</u> <u>Mother</u> <u>Goose</u>. New York: Watts,
     1964.

          A delightful collection including the most popular Mother
     Goose rhymes. Illustrations are bright and original. (P)

Wood, Ray. <u>The</u> <u>American</u> <u>Mother</u> <u>Goose</u>. New York: Lippincott, 1940.

          American pioneers made up these rhymes to tell to their
     children. Modern day youngsters will also enjoy them. The
     illustrations capture the spirit of the rhymes perfectly. (I)

Puzzles

<u>Storybook</u> <u>Puzzles</u>. Playskool, 4501 W. Augusta Blvd., Chicago, Ill. 60651.

          A variety of wooden puzzles with 10 to 15 pieces based on
     Mother Goose rhymes and nursery stories are available from Play-
     skool. Titles include "Humpty-Dumpty," "Rub-a-Dub-Dub," "Old
     Woman in the Shoe," and "Little Red Riding Hood."

MIMING and DRAMATIZING

WITH PUPPETS

Defining Terms

At this level the student will develop greatly--to the level of actively carrying a character through a story fairly much on his/her own! There are two modes which interest us in this chapter.

The first we'll call "miming," where the student is responsible for moving the puppet through the story actions while the librarian/teacher narrates the story.

The second mode is called "dramatizing," because the student
is responsible for both puppet movements and dialogue, as an actor
is responsible for the complete actions and dialogue of a character
in a drama.

From Mime   To develop a puppet play from "miming" to "dramatizing"
to Drama   is very easy. In miming the narrator says everything,
            including dialogue. To write a script for "dramatiz-
ing," you merely give the dialogue to the puppet character.

116

<u>Miming</u>. Narrator: The lion came in. "What are you doing with that

                     sword, Mouse?" he asked.

<u>Dramatizing</u>. Narrator: The lion came in.

                Lion Puppet: "What are you doing with that sword, Mouse?"

There are innumerable stories suitable to both "miming" and "dramatizing" with puppets. A few include: <u>Mushroom in the Rain</u>, <u>The Great Big Enormous Turnip</u>, <u>The Bremen-town Musicians</u>, <u>The Three Billy Goats Gruff</u>, and <u>Henny Penny</u>.

Student Goals With both "miming" and "dramatizing," learning goals are similar: sequencing one's puppet character with others, listening to narration/dialogue with understanding, and matching puppet action to narration/dialogue. In addition, "dramatizing" includes the student learning and saying his/her puppet's dialogue. As

117

always, retarded students will achieve at different levels, and each
student's progress must be measured by his/her abilities.

Librarian/   In "mime" the adult will provide the narration

Teacher   and dialogue of the story. In order to increase

Responsibility   comprehension, the librarian/teacher should have
the play run through from beginning to end as soon as possible. Of
course, you should expect the students to have some rough spots and you
should help them while still promoting the carry-through of the story.

118

In "dramatizing" a story the adult responsibility becomes much greater in preparation even though his/her direct participation in the play becomes considerably lessened. The reason is that a dialogue script suitable for mentally handicapped students must first be carefully prepared. No mean task!

Turning a Story into a Puppet Play

Written Plan There is much forethought necessary to planning a puppet play for mentally retarded students. With regular students, a teacher can make a change, tell the students, and they generally will understand and remember. Not so with handicapped students.

Everything must be firmly set in your own mind (and eventually on paper) so that you are consistent in directing your students. For example, the space designated the "stage" must be set, points of entering and exiting decided and named, desired movements of puppets during

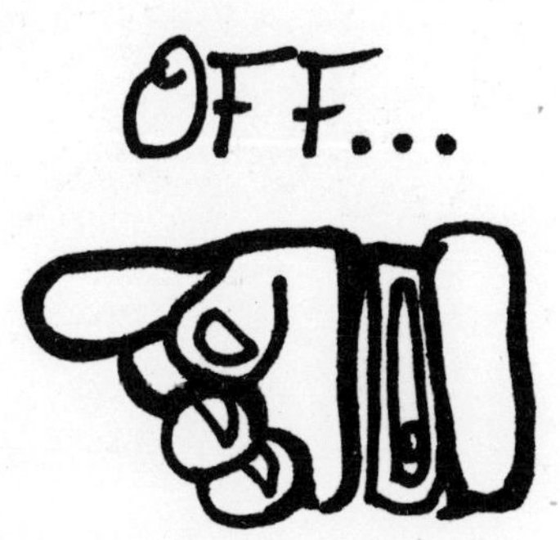

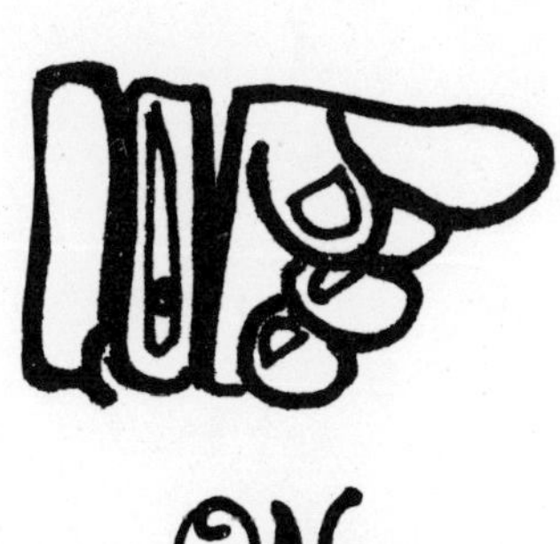

narration/dialogue known, etc. You can imagine how quickly confused
your students could become if you change any of the above.

Thus the need for a written plan!

**Main
Steps**
Briefly, there are four concerns in writing or adapting a
story into a puppet play.

a)   selecting an appropriate story

b)   writing narration-action plan for miming
writing a dialogue-action plan for dramatizing

c)   working out each character's action within the stage area

d)   deciding upon and making appropriate puppets

Selecting
a Story

When deciding upon a story, keep the selection factors
mentioned in the "Selecting Books and Stories" chapter
in mind, for you'll want to prepare the students by
sharing a picture book or an oral story with them first. Such important
factors include: maturity of content, interest level, and simple plot.

Narration and dialogue should be simple or capable of being
simplified without too much bother on your part. On the other hand,
with practice you'll see how easy it will become to turn even the most
complicated narration or dialogue into something simple that your students will understand!

Narrative/
Dialogue
Action

Writing the adaptation may initially be a little
time-consuming. Recall that for "miming" all that
is required is the narration which you will be saying, and the puppet actions which the students will be performing.
Often your only concern will be excluding unessential descriptions from
your script. In more wordy texts, you may have to shorten sentences
or eliminate sentences altogether.

When dramatization of a play is desired, dialogue by the student
should be comprehensible, realistic, and brief enough for the student
to remember without undue stress. You'll want to use strong words in

short sentences that will be meaningful as well as easy to remember.

For example, "I would like to know where your sword is, Mr. Tiger?"

is wordy and weak in comparison to "Where is your sword, Tiger?"

No constructed stage is necessary. Designate the space of the floor which is to serve as the "stage." Let your students know which is to be the "left side" or the "left stage," and which is to be called "right side" or the "right stage." If directionality is a problem, designate the left and right by a nearby common object, e.g., "door side." Place your non-participant "watchers" in a semi-circle or in a three-sided formation around the stage area.

When you begin preparing your written plan, you'll have to know from which side your characters will enter and exit.

Examples   Note the examples, "The Big Turnip" and "Mushroom in the
Rain" in this chapter. Both are easily adapted from the
original stories into puppet plays.

Characters   Writing down directions pertaining to movement helps
And   to keep your students from becoming confused by con-
Actions   flicting or changing directions. Such written
instructions are included under "Characters On-Stage," and "Puppet Actions,"
in the written plan.

Narrative Example: "Mushroom in the Rain"

An adaptation of Mirra Ginsburg's <u>Mushroom</u> <u>in</u> <u>the</u> <u>Rain</u> (Collier
Books, 1974) follows. There are a few words on each page of the book
which can be dropped when adapting it for a puppet play for handicapped
students. For the purpose of lessening the number of characters, we
also omitted the last character in the book--the frog!

<u>Narration</u>	<u>Characters</u> <u>on</u> <u>Stage</u>	<u>Puppet</u> <u>Actions</u>
One day an ant was caught in the rain.	Ant--enters left	Ant tries hiding under leaf, grass
"Where can I hide?" the Ant cried. "It is raining so hard!"	Ant	Ant spies mushroom (an umbrella in closed position)

He saw a tiny mushroom and hid under it.

Ant

Ant squeezes under mushroom

A wet butterfly crawled up to the mushroom. "Cousin Ant, let me come in from the rain."

Butterfly--enters left
Ant

Butterfly tries to keep rain off self by spreading wings

"There's barely room enough for me. But come on," said Ant.

Ant
Butterfly

Ant beckons Butterfly beneath the umbrella

A mouse ran up. "Let me under the mushroom. I'm drenched to the bone."

Mouse--enters left
Butterfly
Ant

Mouse looks up at sky, pushes self under mush-room; but others push him out

"Well," said Butterfly,
"there's hardly room
for us two. But come
on in."

A little sparrow hop-
ped up to the mush-
room. "Let me under
to dry out."

Butterfly
Mouse
Ant

Sparrow--enters right
Butterfly
Mouse
Ant

Mouse excitedly
squeezes under mush-
room

Sparrow hops about
front stage while
talking

"Well, we've hardly
room for ourselves.
But come in," said
Mouse.

Then a rabbit hopped
up to the mushroom.
"Oh, hide me! A fox
is chasing me!"

Mouse
Sparrow
Butterfly
Ant

Rabbit--enters right
Sparrow
Butterfly
Mouse
Ant

Sparrow squeezes
under mushroom

Rabbit runs back and
forth on stage, wring-
ing hands

"Poor Rabbit," said
Ant. "Let's crowd
ourselves a little
more and take him
in."

Ant
Rabbit
Sparrow
Butterfly
Mouse

All grumble but
squeeze together;
Rabbit dives in

As soon as they hid
Rabbit, the fox came
running. "Where's
that Rabbit, I smell
Rabbit around here."

Fox--enters right
Rabbit
Sparrow
Butterfly
Mouse
Ant

Fox sniffs at side of
mushroom

"Don't be silly, Fox.
There's no room for a
big animal like a
rabbit to hide under
this little mushroom!"
said Ant.

Ant
Fox
Rabbit
Sparrow
Butterfly
Mouse

Ant shakes finger at
Fox while speaking

Fox walked around the
mushroom, sniffing.
But he couldn't see
Rabbit. "You're right,"
said Fox. "There are so
many under that mush-
room that Rabbit
couldn't be there too."

Fox--exits left
Rabbit
Ant
Sparrow
Butterfly
Mouse

Fox runs around mush-
room and then exits
left

"The rain has stopped,"
yelled Mouse. And
everybody came out.

Mouse
Rabbit
Ant
Sparrow
Butterfly

Animals come out and
stretch

Rabbit looked at all
the animals and at
the mushroom. "How
did we all fit under
such a little mush-
room?" asked Rabbit.

Rabbit
Ant
Sparrow
Butterfly
Mouse

Rabbit stands in front
of mushroom; others
divided on sides of
mushroom

"I know!" said Sparrow.
"Rain makes a mushroom
grow."

Ant
Rabbit
Sparrow
Butterfly
Mouse

All animals bow and
exit

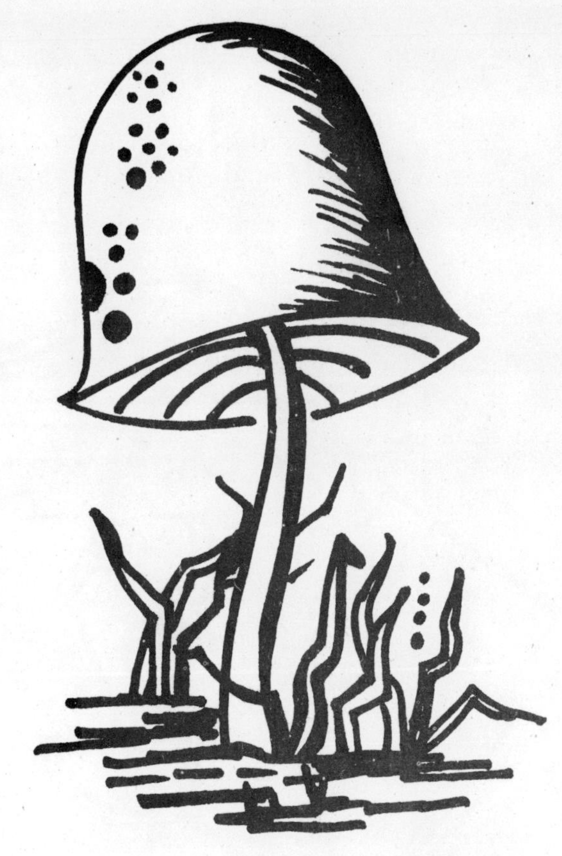

Adding Simple Body Features

A delightful way of making "Mushroom in the Rain" fun and meaning-ful is to let your students actually be the story characters. To distinguish players, have each student make the outstanding feature of his character, for example, the ant can wear antennae, the rabbit can wear long ears, etc.

To Make   For making "body features," have on hand a variety of materials.

-egg cartons   -tissue paper
-clothes hangers   -string
-cardboard   -Elmer's glue
-construction paper   -scissors
-felt and yarn pieces -stapler
                       -crayons

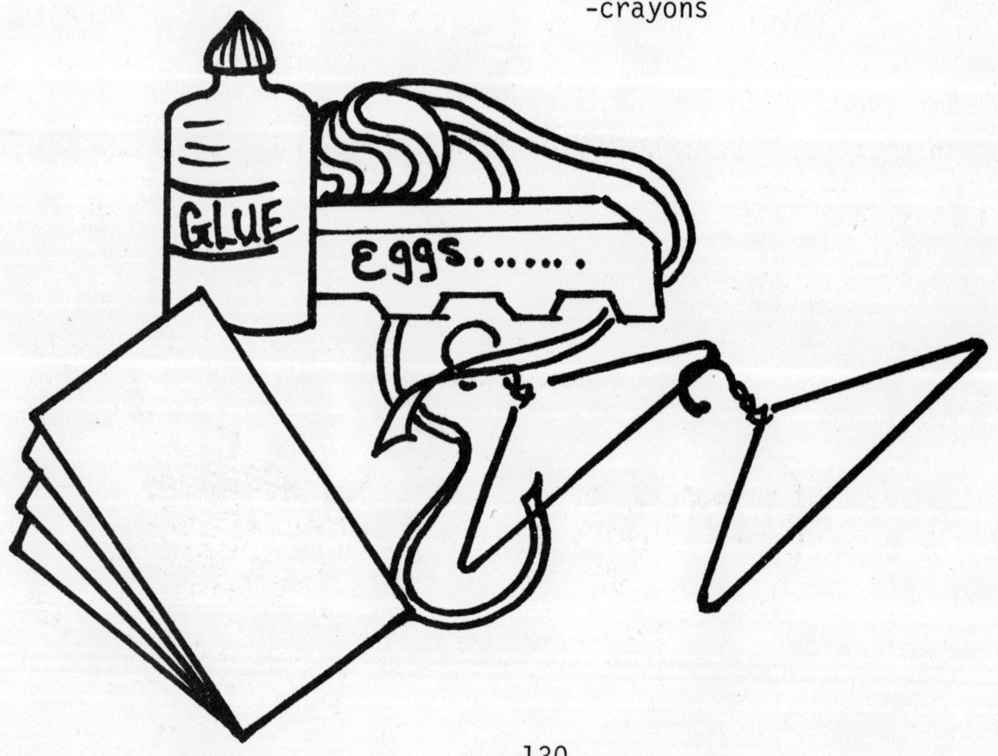

Introduce the idea of making body features by asking
what the students think of in terms of body parts when
they imagine a lion, a mouse, etc. Explain that they
will be assigned an animal from the story, and that they are to choose
the body part that will help distinguish that animal from all others.

To help younger students clarify their thinking you may have to
talk to them about their animal and plans for making the body part. Be
sure to be accepting of what they tell you.

Dialogue Example: "The Big Turnip"

A dialogue-action plan allows the student to participate more fully by making him/her responsible for the
dialogue of a puppet. However, as you'll note in this
example, there is still room for a narrator--at the beginning for introducing a story and later for preparing the entrance of a new character.

In this traditional Russian folktale of the turnip, we have empha-
sized important points to help the understanding of mentally handicapped
youngsters.

131

<table>
<tr><td><u>Speaker</u></td><td><u>Characters</u> <u>on</u> <u>Stage</u></td><td><u>Puppet</u> <u>Actions</u></td></tr>
<tr><td>Narrator: Long, long ago, there was an Old Man. One day he planted a turnip seed.</td><td>Old Man--enters left</td><td>Old Man plants seed on overturned box (garden) Old man--exit right</td></tr>
</table>

<table>
<tr><td>Narrator: That turnip grew large and grew big. Soon it was the biggest turnip in the whole world. Old Man came to pick the turnip.</td><td>Turnip--grows from overturned box, bigger and bigger</td><td>Turnip is pushed up from box by student</td></tr>
</table>

Old Man: "I'll pull this big turnip. Then Wife and I will have turnip pie all winter.	Old Man--enters left	Jumps up and down excitedly
Narrator: Old Man pulled. But he couldn't pull that turnip out. So he called his wife.	Old Man	Tries to pull turnip, but can't
Old Man: "Wife, come help me pull this big turnip. Then we shall have turnip pie."	Old Man	Beckons to left entrance
Narrator: Wife came. Old Man and Wife pulled and pulled. But they couldn't pull that turnip out. So Wife called the dog.	Wife--enters left Old Man	Hang onto one another and pull

Wife: "Dog, come help us pull this turnip. Then we shall have turnip pie."	Dog--enters left Wife Old Man	Wife beckons toward left entrance
Narrator: Dog came. Dog, Wife and Old Man pulled and pulled. But they couldn't pull that turnip out. So Dog called the cat.	Dog Wife Old Man	Hang onto one another and pull
Dog: "Cat, come help us pull this turnip. Then we shall have turnip pie."	Cat--enters left Dog Wife Old Man	Dog beckons toward left entrance

Narrator: Cat came.
Cat, Dog, Wife and
Old Man pulled and
pulled. But they
couldn't pull that
turnip out. So Cat
called the mouse.

Cat   Hang onto one another
Dog   and pull
Wife
Old Man

Cat: "Mouse, come
help us pull this
turnip. Then we
shall have turnip
pie."

Cat   Cat beckons toward right
Dog   entrance
Wife
Old Man

Narrator: Mouse
came. But the
others just laughed.
Then Dog spoke out.

Mouse--enters right   Mouse is surrounded by
Cat   others who laugh
Dog   uproariously
Wife
Old Man

Dog: "If all of us
big folk can't pull
out this turnip, how
can a little mouse
like you help?"

Dog   Dog points to mouse,
Mouse   waves arms
Cat
Wife
Old Man

Narrator: Little
Mouse spoke to Dog.

Mouse: "Just wait.
Maybe my little bit
of help is just what
you all need!"

Mouse   Mouse points hand at
Cat   Dog, then goes to end
Dog   line
Wife
Old Man

Narrator: Mouse, Cat, Dog, Wife, and Old Man pulled and pulled. And as they pulled they counted.	Mouse Cat Dog Wife Old Man	Hang onto one another and pull
Everybody: "One, two, three!"	Mouse Dog Cat Wife Old Man	Back and forth motion of pulling hard; all tumble backwards on "three," as all count, "1, 2, 3!"
Narrator: And everyone fell backwards. But that big turnip came out! Mouse was very pleased.	Mouse Dog Cat Wife Old Man	Mouse gets up from floor and jumps around excitedly
Mouse: "See! Every little bit of help counts!"	Mouse Cat Dog Wife Old Man	Mouse speaks to others who stay on floor
Everybody: "Hooray for Mouse! Hooray for Mouse!"	Mouse Cat Dog Wife Old Man	Others get up and cheer Mouse

Dialogue   The teaching of the puppet's dialogue can be a bit of a

problem if you demand perfection. It's just not going

to happen. Nor should it! Since comprehension and fun

are the reasons for doing educational puppetry, you have to be down-to-

earth on this matter.

If the students approximate the dialogue in their own words, that's

a good indication of success! For that means they're understanding

what's happening and can express it without wasting time in memorizing.

After all, isn't that what being creative and expressive is all

about?

**Giving
Parts**   "The Big Turnip" is an easy story to start with in creat-

ing dialogue with puppets. Character actions are simple

and sequential throughout. Nevertheless, give the first

character, the Old Man, to a more able student, since the first character

usually has less cues to rely on in doing puppet actions. Your other

students will have more visual help for their parts if someone else goes

before them.

Cues   There are many cues you can give to your students initially,

and their use should be geared to individual needs. For

example, Cat goes on stage when Dog calls his name.

Some students will pick up the visual and verbal cues without being

told; others will need to have cues pinpointed for them. Again, this

is an opportunity to individualize your lesson in teaching sequence and
use of cues according to your students' abilities. As with any literature and the mentally handicapped, fun and understanding are the
important elements to be learned, not the dramatic perfection of the
play!

Making Felt Hand Puppets

Hand puppets made from felt are simply and easily made. Intermediate and older students should have little trouble with hand puppet
construction, as long as you're present to direct and encourage. Primary children will most likely be able to complete only "finishing
touches" on hand puppets. Still, this will give them a sense of participation in the creative process. Keep in mind that some students at
every level will need to have more done for them than others.

**Materials
Needed**
To make a felt hand puppet, have the following
materials ready.

-felt pieces (two cutouts needed per puppet)
-felt and yarn bits
-needle and thread
-Elmer's glue
-stapler
-scissors
-tissue paper

Group Process   Begin, as usual, by reading the picture book several times through to your students. Explain the idea of a "talking puppet play" to your students, and the responsibility of everyone involved.

Show an example of a felt puppet and how to manipulate it. Express the idea that it is a more difficult puppet to make and, therefore, it will require clear understanding and patience on their part. Take some time to let the students try on the puppet.

Discuss the different characters in the story and then distribute

responsibility of parts

and making of puppets.

<table>
<tr><td>Making
Procedures</td><td>Take the group through the following steps.</td></tr>
<tr><td></td><td>a) Trace the basic puppet pattern onto a piece of
folded tissue paper. Cut the coupled tissue
pattern.</td></tr>
</table>

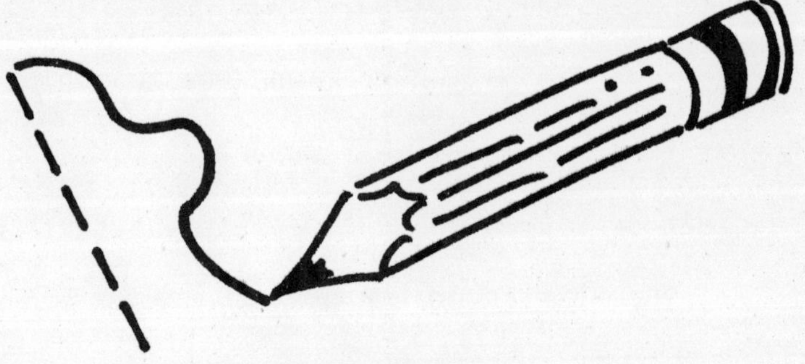

140

Felt
Puppet
Pattern ...
Trace
Cut
Glue and
Decorate ...

b) Open the pattern and place it over two pieces of felt. In
   this way, the student will be cutting both back and front
   parts of the puppet at the same time, and the parts will be
   alike. Cut both pieces at one time.

c) Glue, sew, or staple the puppet pieces along the outer edge.
   (Sewing is most difficult.)

d) Add puppet features which are characteristic of your animal
   or person (e.g., long ears for Dog, hat for Old Man, etc.).

<table>
<tr><td>

Alternate

Puppet

Type

</td><td>

Also suited to this story is the sock puppet, which is easy to make and can be made by even the youngest student. Merely take an old sock, add desired fea-

</td></tr>
</table>

tures of yarn, felt scraps, and egg cartons. Now you're set to go!

Thin cardboard may help catch the characters' telltale features in

the making of ears and noses.

> Whatever your students' puppets look like in reality is less important than the process of creating and learn-ing!

Appropriate Puppets

Deciding what kind of puppets to make for which play is a fun exercise! Factors to consider include:

a) Character of the puppet--is the puppet's character seen by you and your students as small and dainty or large and gruff.

b) Kinds of actions puppet will have to make--a large action as the "trip-trap" of the Big Billy Goat Gruff is more convincing when performed by a big puppet rather than a smaller one.

c) Amount of time available for students to make puppets--paper-plate puppets are quicker and easier to make than felt hand puppets.

d) Amount of use and wear-and-tear--more durable puppets include felt hand puppets while paper-bag puppets will have a limited lifetime.

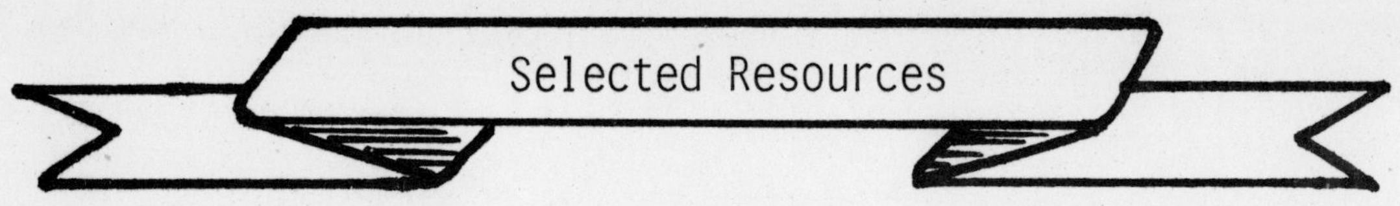

(P) - primary child, (I) - intermediate child, (E) - elementary child

Asbjornsen, P. D. The Three Billy Goats Gruff. Illus. by Marcia
     Brown. New York: Harcourt, Brace, Jovanovich, 1957.

     Wonderful folktale by Asbjornsen with some introduction
necessary, but text perfect as is. Many opportunities to include
sounds ("trip-trap") and chorus parts ("Who's that tripping over
my bridge?"). (E)

Brown, Marcia. Stone Soup. New York: Charles Scribner's Sons, 1947.

     An old favorite but requires text adaptation and more than
one sitting to complete. Review of happenings necessary for
understanding. (I)

Dayrell, Elphinstone. Why the Sun and the Moon Live in the Sky. Boston:
     Houghton Mifflin, 1968.

     An African why story using masked characters to explain a
physical phenomenon. The sun and the moon live in the sky
because the water creatures crowded them out of their home on
earth. (E)

De Regniers, Beatrice. Willy O'Dwyer Jumped in the Fire. New York:
     Atheneum, 1968.

     Good illustrations coupled with a simple, rhyming text make
this book useful for beginning drama activities. Several opportunities for participation. (P)

Eastman, P. D. <u>Are You My Mother</u>? New York: Beginner Books, 1960.

      While searching for its mother, a baby bird meets a variety of unusual characters, including an airplane and a "snort." You can play the part of the baby bird as well as narrate the story. (E)

Galdone, Paul. <u>The Three Bears</u>. New York: Seabury, 1972.

      Large, clear illustrations make this a good version to use when planning the dramatization of the story. Also by the same illustrator <u>The Three Little Pigs</u> (1970). (P)

Ginsburg, Mirra. <u>Mushroom in the Rain</u>. New York: Macmillan, 1972.

      An adaptation of a Russian folktale about animals hiding under a mushroom to stay dry. Text is appropriate and pictures perfect. Good sequences of happenings, animals to point out, and concepts to learn. (I)

Hutchins, Pat. <u>Rosie's Walk</u>. New York: Macmillan, 1968.

      Children can use puppets to mime the adventures of a chicken chased by a fox around the farmyard. (P)

Krum, Charlotte. <u>The Four Riders</u>. Chicago: Wilcox & Follett, 1953.

      The journey of a horse which accepts a variety of riders provides an opportunity for individual children to be responsible for one puppet throughout the story. (I)

Tolstoy, Alexi. <u>The Great Big Enormous Turnip</u>. New York: Watts, 1969.

      The attempts of an old man, his wife, and several animals to pull up a turnip are unsuccessful until a mouse lends a helping hand. (E)

Wildsmith, Brian. <u>The</u> <u>Hare</u> <u>and</u> <u>the</u> <u>Tortoise</u>. New York: Watts, 1966.

     This popular fable about a slow but steady tortoise who
beats the hare in a race is an excellent story for beginning
drama participation. (I)

Young, Ed. <u>The</u> <u>Lion</u> <u>and</u> <u>the</u> <u>Mouse</u>. Garden City, New York: Doubleday,
    1979.

     Aesop's fable with graceful illustrations but a moral that
will need to be discussed for understanding. Try other examples,
e.g., "Even though a big person can move a table alone, a small
person can hold the door." Children can use puppets to dramatize
in pairs as you narrate. (I)

PRESENTING BIOGRAPHIES

WITH PUPPETS

For the older student, incidents in the lives of famous persons can be made memorable through the use of puppets. The first step is to select people whom you know will interest intermediate students-- sports figures, presidents, entertainers from film and television. Muhammad Ali, Nadia Comaneci, and John Travolta come easily to mind.

Historical Figures
History is full of noteworthy heroes and cowards, and the special student should have an introduction to them. Basic history must include Columbus, Lincoln, and Washington. What better way than to use puppets to repre- sent these historical figures! And there are thousands of others.

<table>
<tr><td>

**Local
Figures**

</td><td>

Most mentally handicapped youth will acquire interest in local affairs when presented puppet introductions within the classroom or library! Once the student has acquired

</td></tr>
</table>

a little knowledge about local persons, he/she will continue to learn of

them through television and conversation.

<table>
<tr><td>

**Finding a
Celebrity**

</td><td>

Selecting a person whose life interests your students is quite simple. The more difficult decision is choosing an incident or event in that person's life

</td></tr>
</table>

to share with your students. We suggest that you think of the qualities

of that famous person which you would like to pass on to your students,

and then to choose an incident demonstrating at least one of those

qualities.

For example, Buffalo Bill exhibited courage, cunning and humor

throughout his life. Therefore, a biographic play of Buffalo Bill

would certainly illustrate at least one of these qualities.

<table>
<tr><td>

**Literary
License**

</td><td>

Generally, biographical incidents presented in children's non-fiction are not detailed in dialogue. Therefore,

</td></tr>
</table>

you can assume some literary license in formulating appropriate dialogue and action for your play.

Imagine
Dialogue
A picture or brief mention of an occurrence can help
you imagine or invent dialogue that might have accom-
panied that event. For example, an encounter between
Buffalo Bill and two would-be bandits serves as the basis for the
dialogue-action play which follows. And while we have no means of
knowing what conversation actually did occur, the dialogue we decided
upon does illustrate the qualities which history attributes to Buffalo
Bill Cody.

"Buffalo Bill and the Outlaws"
(An Overhead Shadow Play)

Action	Dialogue
<u>Lights out.</u> Mail pouch on bottom left side of overhead projector. <u>Lights on.</u> Move mail pouch slowly toward middle. Pony enters from left and nudges pouch onto his back. Pony gallops off screen.	Narrator: In 1860 the Pony Express was the fastest way to send mail across the West.

Small figure of Buffalo Bill on
horseback crosses screen from
left side.

Narrator: One of the most famous
riders for the Pony Express was
Buffalo Bill Cody. When Buffalo
Bill was a young Pony Express rider,
he was held up by outlaws.

<u>Lights</u> <u>out</u>.

Bill: Giddiup, Scout.

<u>Lights</u> <u>on</u>. Bill on center
screen. Jake jumps down in
front of Bill's horse, as out
of a tree. (Pouch on horse.)

Jake: Reach for the sky.

Sam jumps down in back of
Bill's horse.

Sam: And no funny business, Son!

152

Bill's horse moves slightly
in a nervous manner.

Sam shakes his gun threat-
eningly.

Jake walks closer to Bill.

Bill: What can I do for you,
Sirs?

Sam: We heard that the mail pouch
you're carrying has plenty of money
in it.

Jake: That's right. So hand over
the mail pouch.

Bill hits Jake over the head
with the mail pouch. Jake
falls to the ground.

Sam approaches Bill from behind
to grab him.

Bill: Why sure. Please help yourself!

Sam: What! I'll show you, you
young whippersnapper.

Scout (horse) whinnies and
rears his legs, kicking Sam
to the ground.

Jake gets up, retrieves the
mail pouch and gives it to
Bill.

Bill: Up, Scout!

Jake: Buffalo Bill, you let us
go and we won't bother you.

Jake and Sam scurry off-stage.

Bill rides off-stage right.
<u>Lights</u> <u>out</u>.

<u>Lights</u> <u>on</u>. Grown-up Buffalo
Bill on horseback rides across
the stage from right. <u>Lights</u>
<u>out</u>.

Bill: You two get along before I
get mad.

Bill: Now with those bandits gone,
I better get this Pony Express mail
on its way!

Narrator: When Buffalo Bill got
older, he became famous by putting
together a cowboy and Indian circus
called "The Wild West Show."

The End

Shadow
Puppets

An excellent choice for this action play would be overhead projector shadow puppets. "Shadow puppets" are
called such because of the black shadow cast by the thin
cardboard or oaktag puppets when placed on an overhead projector. Older
students find this puppet type fascinating and quickly learn the techniques of making and operating this puppet.

Making Overhead Shadow Puppets

Uses

This type of puppet is especially useful when there is
plenty of action, or movement on and off stage. Another
valuable use is to show the numerous accomplishments of
events which have occurred in one person's life, as for example, the
important events of a President from childhood through middle-age.

To make this puppet (e.g., Buffalo Bill), you'll

need the following:

-light oaktag or construction paper
-thin wooden skewers or straws
-masking tape
-scissors
-overhead projector and screen

When making original shadow puppets, one of the first

things to determine is the size of puppets needed. The

reason for this is that your "stage" is the glass surface

of the overhead projector. This glass surface is quite small and,

therefore, your puppets need to be relatively small cutouts. To help

in determining the appropriate size of the puppet cutouts, determine

from the script the maximum amount of puppets on stage at any one time,

and experiment with sizes for those puppets.

Buffalo
Bill
Patterns

The patterns included within the script may be traced by students and used in making puppets for "Buffalo Bill and the Outlaws." Use tracing paper to transfer the outlines from the book to oaktag or construction paper. Cut the oaktag with scissors, making sure that the shapes are cleanly cut and well-defined.

Attach
Skewers

Take each puppet cutout and attach a skewer or straw by means of masking tape. This will serve as the "handle" of the puppet.

Hints for
Manipulation

1) Very little actual movement is required once the puppet is onstage. Small actual movements will appear large on the standing screen.

2) Arrange your puppets and props in order of appearance. It's generally easier to have no more than two persons maneuver the puppets.

3) Let the dialogue and narration be said by students other than the puppeteers.

4) To help students with directionality, tape little "left" and "right" signs to the appropriate sides of the projector as the student faces it and from which he/she will be manipulating the puppets.

Advantages   There are several advantages to using biographical
              puppet plays with your students, particularly older
              students. The intermediate student will view puppets
with great seriousness, as well as the subject matter being taught.
Likewise will the student's esteem be heightened due to the interest
he/she will receive from average students over this new and interesting
media form.

Puppets   In this case as in all cases, the outcome of educational
And   puppetry should be learning, creating, and enjoying.
Students   Puppets in education could be the needed ingredient
toward revitalizing your student's interest in learning and enjoying
the world of literature.

Bibliography   "Selected Resources" in this chapter is a list of
                children's and young adults' biographies which are
                meant to serve as references for the librarian/
teacher. These will help in formulating biographical plays. Students
may enjoy the illustrations and photographs after viewing the play.

(P) - primary child, (I) - intermediate child, (E) - elementary child

Anderson, La Vere. Sitting Bull. Champaign, Ill.: Garrard, 1970.

     The disappearing Indian way of life is vividly portrayed in this simply written story of a great Sioux Chief. (I)

Aulaire, Ingri d'. Buffalo Bill. Garden City, NY: Doubleday, 1952.

     The excitement and challenge of the Wild West are interwoven throughout this beautifully illustrated version of the life of Buffalo Bill Cody. (I)

Aulaire, Ingri d'. Pocahontas. Garden City, NY: Doubleday, 1946.

     The story of one of America's first heroines, Pocahontas, whose life was interwoven with interesting adventures and people, including Powhatan, Captain John Smith, and the Queen of England.

Edwards, Anne. The Great Houdini. New York: Putnam, 1977.

     The fascinating life of the master magician and escape artist, Harry Houdini, unfolds in this "See and Read Biography." (I)

Edwards, Audrey. Picture Life of Muhammad Ali. New York: Watts, 1976.

     Splendid photographs on every page highlight this life story of a unique sports figure. Other people presented in this "Picture Life Books" series which use many pictures coupled with simple text include: Jimmy Carter; Stevie Wonder; Martin Luther King, Jr. (I)

Fritz, Jean. <u>And Then What Happened, Paul Revere?</u> New York: Coward,
    McCann & Geoghegan, 1973.

        Amusing account of the life of Paul Revere which includes
    many details about his domestic affairs and his life as a crafts-
    man. (I)

Grant, Matthew G. <u>Buffalo Bill of the Wild West</u>. Chicago: Children's
    Press, 1974.

        The many careers of a unique and colorful personality are
    briefly described in this book from the "Gallery of Great Americans
    Series." Other titles describe "Women of America," "War Heroes of
    America," "Explorers of America," and "Frontiersmen of America."
    (I)

Robinson, Nancy. <u>Janet Guthrie: Race Car Driver</u>. Chicago: Children's
    Press, 1979.

        The determination of Janet to succeeed in a sport dominated
    by men is seen against the exciting backdrop of the auto racing
    world. Other "Sports Stars" books include: Steve Garvey; Nancy
    Lopez; and Walter Payton. (I)